THE
FOUNDATIONS
OF
KNOWLEDGE

CENTRAL ISSUES IN PHILOSOPHY SERIES

BARUCH A. BRODY
series editor

edited by

CHARLES LANDESMAN
Hunter College

THE

FOUNDATIONS

OF

KNOWLEDGE

Prentice-Hall, Inc., Englewood Cliffs, New Jersey

Library of Congress Catalog Card Number: 76–117012

Printed in the United States of America

C 13–329557–5
P 13–329540–0

Current Printing (last digit):

10 9 8 7 6 5 4 3 2 1

PRENTICE-HALL INTERNATIONAL, INC., London
PRENTICE-HALL OF AUSTRALIA, PTY. LTD., Sydney
PRENTICE-HALL OF CANADA, LTD., Toronto
PRENTICE-HALL OF INDIA PRIVATE LIMITED, New Delhi
PRENTICE-HALL OF JAPAN, INC., Tokyo

Foreword

The Central Issues in Philosophy series is based upon the conviction that the best way to teach philosophy to introductory students is to experience or to *do* philosophy with them. The basic unit of philosophical investigation is the particular problem, and not the area or the historical figure. Therefore, this series consists of sets of readings organised around well-defined, manageable problems. All other things being equal, problems that are of interest and relevance to the student have been chosen.

Each volume contains an introduction that clearly defines the problem and sets out the alternative positions that have been taken. The selections are chosen and arranged in such a way as to take the student through the dialectic of the problem; each reading, besides presenting a particular point of view, criticizes the points of view set out earlier.

Although no attempt has been made to introduce the student in a systematic way to the history of philosophy, classical selections relevant to the development of the problem have been included. As a side benefit, the student will therefore come to see the continuity, as well as the breaks, between classical and contemporary thought. But in no case will a selection be included merely for its historical significance; clarity of expression and systematic significance are the main criteria for selection.

BARUCH A. BRODY

Contents

Introduction

This volume contains writings by ten authors—both classical and contemporary—presenting their opinions on the fundamental problem of the philosophy of knowledge or epistemology, which is the problem of determination of the nature and foundations of knowledge. The selections were chosen on the basis of their historical importance and influence, and relevance to contemporary issues and debates in epistemology. A careful study of these articles will provide the reader with the necessary background, both historical and conceptual, to develop an understanding of the problems involved. This introduction is intended to present the reader with a definition of epistemology and with a survey of the major topics discussed in the selections that follow.

EPISTEMOLOGY. That more than one type of knowledge exists becomes apparent in considering the following sentences:

(1) Tom knows how to swim.
(2) Tom knows that water freezes when the temperature drops below 32°F.

In the first sentence, the kind of knowledge Tom has is *knowing how* to do something, which is a case of *practical knowledge*. In the second, Tom *knows that* something is so. He knows the truth of a certain proposition, namely, the proposition that water freezes when the temperature drops below 32° F. This is a case of *propositional knowledge*. These two types of knowledge are often associated with one another. Learning a skill often requires learning certain truths, as when a medical student studies chemistry and biology; and almost invariably the learning of truths presupposes certain skills, such as knowing how to read or to interpret speech. Despite these connections, epistemology has been concerned mostly with propositional knowledge: with the question how we know something to be true or false.[1]

A person may claim to know something without using the word "know." He may say, for example, "I *remember* that the key is in my desk drawer" or "I *see* that the key is in my desk drawer." The words "remember" and "see," along with such other words as "perceive," "hear," and "recognize" are often used to imply the possession of propositional knowledge. Seeing, remembering, hearing, and recognizing in such cases can be thought of as *forms of knowledge* or as ways of acquiring knowledge.

Epistemology is the study of knowledge and its various forms. It is important, however, to initially sequester the different perspectives of studying knowledge. It is generally agreed that the perspective of the psychology of knowledge must be distinguished from the philosophy of knowledge. To explain this distinction, let us consider a situation where Tom claims to know a particular jacket is blue. Suppose that John asks how Tom knows it is blue. If John is an experimental psychologist and Tom is his subject in an experiment, the question "How does he know that?" can be interpreted as: "What are the facts about Tom and the circumstances in which he is situated which explain his knowing it is blue?" Suppose Tom found it to be blue because he perceived it. John might then investigate such matters as the kind of light reflected from the jacket, the effect of the light waves upon Tom's eyes and his visual system, the passage of the visual signals to his brain, and the influence of his past experience and his present attitudes in the way he responds to the signals. An explanation of this type of a person's knowledge is like a narrative in which each stage provides the causes of the succeeding stages. The construction of such a narrative is aided by knowledge of theories of physics, chemistry, biology, and psychology. In acquiring this knowl-

---

[1] A discussion of the differences between practical and propositional knowledge is contained in Gilbert Ryle, *The Concept of Mind* (London: Hutchinson's University Library, 1949), Chap. ii: "Knowing How and Knowing That."

edge, Tom need not be familiar with the narrative or with the pre-supposed theories.

John may not be an experimental psychologist, however, and may not have any scientific interest in the origin of Tom's knowledge. Suppose rather that John doubts the color of the jacket and desires to know the true color. He asks Tom "How do you know it is blue?" hoping to elicit Tom's *reasons* which *justify* his claiming to know that it is blue. The question "How do you know?" (whose nuances are fully discussed by J. L. Austin in selection 8), when asked under ordinary circumstances, is a request for a justification of a knowledge claim. Unlike the facts of the explanatory narrative, the reasons a person has for thinking he knows something must at some point be capable of being known by that person.

This second way of raising the question "How do you know?" is characteristic of epistemology and distinguishes it from psychology in particular and the empirical sciences in general. While the philosopher may find scientific facts useful and relevant in the course of his inquiry, the question he wishes to answer: "What justifies you in claiming to know that?" is more like the ethical question: "What justifies you in doing that?" than a request for a scientific explanation. A reasonable description of epistemology is *the ethics of belief*.[2]

The interest the philosopher, however, has in knowledge has not yet been precisely focused upon. When he asks someone the question "How do you know that your belief is true?" he is not concerned, as we are in ordinary circumstances, with the particular details of the answer; but rather with the *sort* of answer it is and the way it either succeeds or fails in justifying that *type* of knowledge claim. As asked by the philosopher, the question is Socratic: to elicit the general criteria or principles by which any knowledge claim can be justified. Once the principles are exposed they can be examined to determine the sort of justification to which they are susceptible. Normally we are interested in justifying or criticizing particular knowledge claims by the conscious or unconscious use of principles of justification, which can be termed *epistemic principles*. The focus of interest in ordinary life is on the particular claims to possess

---

[2] A book which is explicitly written from this perspective is Roderick M. Chis-holm's *Perceiving: A Philosophical Study* (Ithaca: Cornell University Press, 1957), especially Part I: "The Ethics of Belief."

knowledge, but in the philosophy of knowledge the principles of justification of knowledge are the objects of attention and analysis.

KNOWLEDGE. Before one undertakes the task of formulating epistemic principles, a problem to be considered is the nature of knowledge. What does it mean to say that someone knows something, that someone has propositional knowledge? What is required to be true for Tom to *know* that water freezes when the temperature drops below 32° F.? At least two conditions in the analysis of knowledge have been recognized by most philosophers who have considered them including C. I. Lewis and Bertrand Russell in selections one and two.[3] First, if Tom really *knows* that water freezes when the temperature drops below 32° F., then it must be *true* that water freezes at that temperature. Knowledge implies the truth of what is known. Therefore, knowledge is a kind of achievement; it is the attainment of truth. If a person claims to know a proposition which is proven false, then he does not know but only *thinks* he knows. Establishing the falsehood of what a person says he knows is one way of criticizing his claim.

Secondly, Tom cannot know that water freezes below 32° F. if he has never entertained or actually disbelieves this proposition. A person who knows a proposition must be in a certain state of mind; he must be sure of it, have confidence in it, believe it, or at least accept it.[4] To have knowledge is at least to have true belief. That true belief is not enough for knowledge has been recognized since the time of Plato. A person may arrive at truth by a lucky guess, by accident, or by the wrong reasons. In these cases we would not say that he possesses knowledge. The problem then is to discover what one has to have in addition to true belief for knowledge to be present. A solution originally suggested by Plato and reiterated by C. I. Lewis (in the first selection) is that *knowledge is a true belief which is justified by a reason or ground.* We may now ask:

---

[3] Plato, in his dialogues *Meno* and *Theaetetus*, seems to have been the first to formulate the two conditions and to understand the particular problem of trying to analyze the concept of propositional knowledge.

[4] That belief is necessary for knowledge has been challenged by E. J. Lemmon in "If I know, do I know that I know?" in *Epistemology, New Essays in the Theory of Knowledge*, ed. Avrum Stroll (New York: Harper & Row, Publishers, 1967), p. 58.

What does it mean for a person's belief to be justified by a reason? A natural answer is that the person has good evidence in its favor. The definition of knowledge can be thus restated: *Knowledge is a true belief for which one has good evidence.* This proposal, natural as it may seem, is subject to at least three criticisms.

First, there are cases in which a person's belief proves to be true, his evidence is good, and yet he does not have knowledge. Consider the case of a box containing four blue and two red marbles. A person justifiably believes that the first marble drawn from the box will be blue because there are more blue than red marbles. If his belief should prove to be true, we would not want to say that he *knew* it would be blue. This criticism can perhaps be avoided by stipulating that the evidence be very strong. But where should the line be drawn? In the second selection Bertrand Russell suggests that a precise definition of knowledge along these lines is not possible since knowledge merges gradually into probable opinion.

Secondly, a plausible statement is that a person has evidence for a belief only if he *knows* the truth of some proposition justifying his belief. Thus, having evidence presupposes having knowledge. Therefore, the definition of knowledge is proven to be circular: knowledge is defined by reference to having evidence which is defined by reference to having knowledge.

In the third place, it seems possible for a person to know something to be true when he has no evidence and when demands for evidence are inappropriate. Is it reasonable to ask a person who knows that he is feeling a sharp pain in his abdomen, that he is imagining a red patch, or that he is raising his arm how *he* knows these things? These would seem to be things that can be *known directly*—the terms *intuition* and *self-evidence* have often been used to describe this type of knowledge. Russell thinks he can define derivative knowledge as true belief inferred validly from what is known intuitively; but he does not succeed in formulating a clear noncircular definition of intuitive knowledge.

The problem of formulating an adequate definition of knowledge is still frequently debated. Attempts have been made to defend the traditional analysis against these criticisms or to qualify it in various ways. The bibliography at the end of this edition lists several of the current contributions in this area.

THE FOUNDATIONS OF KNOWLEDGE. In describing the body of human knowledge, many philosophers used an architectural metaphor; the set of known propositions is like an edifice resting upon foundations which provide it with structural stability. Often the use of this metaphor is justified by a certain argument: an argument of the type called an *infinite regress argument*. This argument was first set forth by Aristotle (in his *Posterior Analytics*, Book I, Chapter 3) and was echoed by Thomas Reid (see the sixth selection). Some matters are known because we are provided with sufficient reasons for them. They are inferred from other propositions. We shall call this *derivative knowledge,* following Russell. According to the infinite regress argument, not all knowledge can be derivative. Suppose, for the sake of argument, that all knowledge is derivative: then any proposition known to be true is based on some other proposition or propositions. These other propositions are based, in turn, on others which are then based on others, *ad infinitum*. Thus, proof or verification can never be terminated, and nothing could ever be known. This conclusion is absurd; the assumption from which it was derived—that all knowledge is derivative—must be false. Other forms of knowledge must also exist: one of which is termed *intuitive knowledge*. Knowledge can thus be divided into two categories—things known intuitively which are the true foundations of knowledge, and things known derivatively by reasoning. This distinction between intuitive and derivative knowledge is made not only by such contemporary philosophers as Russell, but also in their own manner, by Descartes, Locke, and Reid in the included selections.

It is one thing to provide an abstract argument that there must be intuitive knowledge if there is knowledge at all and another thing to provide a method for identifying particular cases of intuitive knowledge. Descartes claims to have discovered such a method with his technique of *theoretical doubt* (see the second part of the third selection). A person may doubt the validity of something he had formerly believed by learning reasons that undercut his earlier belief. For example, I am caused to doubt that all swans have white plumage by reading in an authoritative encyclopedia that black swans inhabit Australia. This doubt will be termed *practical doubt*. Descartes does not attempt to provide us with specific reasons for thinking that certain things are actually false; his is not practical doubt. What he does try to show for a large class of our beliefs is that for all we know they *may* be false. For example, although I now believe that a yellow pencil is in my hand, for all I know I may be dreaming, and a yellow pencil may not be in my hand. When this technique of theoretical doubt is applied to its limits, what is alleged to remain is what is known with absolute certainty. To identify what is known with certainty with intuitive knowledge is only a short step; this identification is characteristic of much traditional epistemology.

In Descartes's hands the method of theoretical doubt cuts rather deeply. He doubts the existence of physical bodies (his own included), the existence of other persons, and even the truth of basic arithmetical equations. If his technique ended here he would be an extreme sceptic. However, he claims to establish with certainty his own existence (see the third part of the third selection), and he also attempts to re-establish on a basis of certainty many of the things he previously doubted. For Descartes, scepticism is a powerful philosophical technique for establishing nonsceptical results. Yet, Descartes does contribute to making scepticism one of the primary problems of modern philosophy by clearly demonstrating that scepticism will result if, accepting the method of doubt, nothing can be found which cannot be doubted; or, even if something certain should be found, the edifice is not properly linked to the foundations. What John Dewey calls "the quest for certainty" became after Descartes one of the primary preoccupations of traditional epistemology.[5]

Even among philosophers who agree that such a thing as certain intuitive knowledge exists, no unanimity is present concerning the types of propositions that can be known intuitively. Some philosophers will admit elementary principles of mathematics and geometry such as: "Two plus three equals five" and "Two straight lines do not enclose an area." Others will accept statements about our sensations and sensory appearances such as: "I am now feeling pain" and "It now appears as if there were a yellow pencil before me." Others will include theological claims such as "God exists" and ethical judgments such as "Pain is evil." Thomas Reid recognizes

---

[5] Dewey's critique of the quest and his pragmatic alternative are contained in his *The Quest for Certainty* (New York: Minton, Balch, and Co., 1929).

the possibility of such disagreements, and in the sixth selection he recommends certain ways of resolving them.

One important and influential theory concerning the nature of the foundations of knowledge is called *empiricism;* its classic formulation occurs in the writings of the British empiricists Locke, Berkeley, and Hume. According to a strict definition of empiricism all intuitive knowledge consists of propositions directly concerning sensory experience: our sensations of sight, hearing, touch, taste, and smell. That all knowledge is *empirical* means that it is either about sensory experience or is derived from propositions about sensory experience. A problem for the empiricist concerns the status of propositions apparently knowable *a priori* or independently of sensory experience such as the truths of mathematics and logic. John Stuart Mill (in his *A System of Logic,* Book II, Chapters 5 and 6, 1843) assumes the position of denying that mathematical truths are *a priori,* and argues that they really are generalizations based on sense experience. Contemporary empiricists—sometimes called *logical positivists*—assert that mathematical truths, though not based on experience, are founded upon definitions or linguistic conventions such as "All triangles have three angles," which is true because of the definition or meaning of the word "triangle." Statements which are true as a result of the meanings of the words used in the sentences which express them are called analytic truths and are alleged not to state facts about the world. Factual or synthetic statements are, according to the empiricist, all empirical.[6] *Rationalism* is the contrary doctrine suggested in some of the writings of Plato, Descartes, Spinoza, and Kant: there are factual propositions, the truth of which can be established *a priori* or independently of experience.[7]

A significant problem within the empiricist tradition is presented

[6] A well-known readable exposition and defense of logical positivism is A. J. Ayer, *Language, Truth, and Logic,* 1936.

[7] A position incompatible with both empiricism and rationalism as they are stated here is one which denies that there is a precise distinction to be drawn between the empirical and the *a priori* and between the analytic and the synthetic. An excellent statement of this position formulated in the tradition of F. H. Bradley and the coherence theory of truth is Brand Blanshard, *The Nature of Thought* (London: George Allen and Unwin, 1939), especially Chap. 30. An influential statement is in Quine's "Two Dogmas of Empiricism" a section of which is contained in the second part of the ninth selection in this anthology.

in the selections by Locke and Berkeley. Locke considers the sense experiences (described by him as ideas of sensation), caused by the impact of physical particles upon the sense organs, as the objects of awareness in perception. When a person sees that something is square, according to this view he is directly aware of the idea or sensation of a square object, and he judges or infers that a square object really exists causing him to have the idea. Since the ideas are taken to represent or to resemble the objects which cause them, Locke's view is sometimes called the *representative theory of perception* and sometimes the *causal theory of perception.*

Locke argues that ideas of sensation are not perfect representations of the true nature of physical bodies. Certain qualities of bodies such as solidity, bulk, extension, shape, and mobility—the *primary qualities*—are represented in ideas as they truly are in bodies. Other qualities such as colors, sounds, odors, tastes, and sensations of temperature—the *secondary qualities*—he states "are nothing in the objects themselves, but powers to produce various sensations in us by their primary qualities." The reason for this distinction is that sensations of colors, sounds and other secondary qualities can be completely explained by the physical influence of bodies upon our sense organs; only primary qualities need to be assumed in bodies to account for their influence. When a person is cut by a sharp knife, he does not ascribe the pain he feels to the knife but to himself; he has the pain, not the knife. A person's direct awareness of a pain is an awareness of something in himself. According to Locke, colors and sounds are generally like pains or bodily sensations. As things directly perceived, they are sensations and hence are subjective; as things in objects, they are merely the powers or capacities of the primary qualities to cause these sensations. Secondary qualities are *merely* causal powers of the primary. Primary qualities have causal powers as well, but their nature is not exhausted by describing the sorts of things they can cause. Locke was under no illusions that his is the view of common sense; he asserts quite explicitly that ordinarily the primary qualities are not distinguished from the secondary qualities in the way they should precisely be, and that secondary qualities "are looked upon as real qualities in the things thus affecting us."

Locke reserves the category of sensitive knowledge for the knowledge about physical bodies acquired by perception. This type does not have the certainty of intuitive nor of demonstrative knowledge. In the selection by Locke, his arguments that scepticism concerning the existence of bodies is not warranted and that our perceptual beliefs truly deserve the title of knowledge are included. Berkeley, however, does not agree. He provides a battery of arguments attempting to show that no valid line of reasoning exists which could carry us from the ideas of sensation to the objects causing them, as alleged by Locke. He explicitly directs his attack against Locke's distinction between primary and secondary qualities, claiming as inconceivable that the former could exist without the latter.

Berkeley does not argue in the interests of scepticism; he does not doubt the existence of physical bodies accepted by common sense. In normal perceptual consciousness, a physical body is not understood as something which merely causes what is directly perceived, but is thought of as being directly perceived. When I perceive the yellow pencil before me, I think of the pencil as directly accessible to my gaze and not as something underlying and causing what I am gazing at. Both Berkeley and Locke agree that what one directly perceives are ideas, but since Berkeley argues against Locke that physical objects are things directly perceived, Berkeley concludes that objects are collections of ideas. Since ideas exist only in so far as they are perceived, Berkeley concludes that objects are mind-dependent: that their existence depends upon a mind perceiving them. Since he is interested in defending common sense against scepticism, to question him about the status of objects not being perceived at some moment of time is appropriate; common sense recognizes that such bodies could exist. One answer, but not the only one that he provides, is the historical source of an important contemporary theory called *phenomenalism:* "The table I write on I say exists; that is, I see and feel it: and if I were out of my study I should say it existed; meaning thereby that if I was in my study I might perceive it, or that some other spirit actually does perceive it." Phenomenalism identifies the perceived physical object with actual and possible sensations; a statement asserting the existence of a physical object implies the existence of sensations that persons are having or that they would have under certain conditions.

The debate between phenomenalism and the representative theory of perception is not one of disagreement about the nature of intuitive knowledge but rather one of disagreement as to how intuitive knowledge leads to derived knowledge, and how the edifice is to be related to the foundation. The phenomenalist is likely to admit only deductive and certain restricted types of inductive reasoning as legitimate ways of passing from one to the other. The advocates of the representative theory will allow a looser variety of inferences to pass from sense experience to things which, though not directly experienced, are postulated as plausible explanations of the flux of our experience.

CONTEMPORARY THEORIES OF THE FOUNDATIONS. While some twentieth century philosophers are interested in refining the view of Descartes, Locke, and Berkeley, and in carrying on in traditional frames of reference, others challenge the basic assumptions of these frames of reference. The selections in the third part are intended to provide the reader with some of the more influential lines of criticism of the tradition.

Each philosopher represented in the third part of this anthology rejects the view that intuitive knowledge consists of propositions known with absolute certainty. This contemporary rejection of a traditional doctrine is presaged in the selections by Reid and Russell who admit that degrees of certainty are present in intuitive knowledge. Austin (in the eighth selection) proffers examples showing that forming mistaken judgments about one's own sense experience is possible. Quine and Goodman (in the ninth and tenth selections) point out that any proposition about one's sense experience may conflict with other propositions and may thus be rejected for good reason. The result of these criticisms is that there is no privileged class of incorrigible statements immune from error and criticism. Both Popper (in the seventh selection) and Quine reject any sharp distinction between observation statements which directly report observed facts and theoretical statements which assert more than is directly given in experience. All statements commit us to more than can be directly observed; perhaps the idea of there being something directly observed is a myth.[8]

If one refuses to enter upon the quest for certainty or thinks that certainty cannot be attained, then one is thereby committed to re-

---

[8] Wilfrid Sellars calls this the "myth of the given." For his criticism of the myth see his *Science, Perception and Reality* (London: Routledge and Kegan Paul, 1963), especially Chap. 5.

ject Descartes's method of doubt as the primary technique of epistemological analysis. J. L. Austin states that from the standpoint of common sense, of what is normally said and done, doubt about the reality of some object must be justified by a specific reason relevant to circumstances at hand. The wholesale doubt characteristic of Descartes' method is not appropriate to common sense modes of verification. That I might have made a mistake, or that what I think I know I really might not know, does not prove that I do not in fact know what I think I know.

The American philosopher Charles Sanders Peirce (1839–1914) was one of the first to develop this type of criticism of Descartes. In a well-known passage he states: "We cannot begin with complete doubt. We must begin with all the prejudices which we actually have when we enter upon the study of philosophy. These prejudices are not to be dispelled by a maxim, for they are things which it does not occur to us *can* be questioned. Hence this initial scepticism will be a mere self-deception and not real doubt; and no one who follows the Cartesian method will ever be satisfied until he has formally recovered all those beliefs which in form he has given up. . . . A person may, it is true, in the course of his studies, find reason to doubt what he began by believing; but in that case he doubts because he has a positive reason for it, and not on account of the Cartesian maxim. Let us not pretend to doubt in philosophy what we do not doubt in our hearts." [9]

The claims that knowledge has foundations, and that intuitive knowledge serves as the reason or evidence for all knowledge have also been subjected to perceptive criticism. One criticism is derived from the rejection of the quest for certainty. If any proposition can possibly be rejected for some good reason, then any proposition might have good reasons in its favor. For example, a person might defend an assertion that he feels a pain in his abdomen by appealing to his past veracity and accuracy in judgments involving some kind of sensory discrimination. Thus, not only do we appeal to the "foundations" to marshall evidence for the "edifice," but the "edi-

---

[9] From Peirce's article "Some Consequences of Four Incapacities" which originally appeared in the *Journal of Speculative Philosophy* (1868) and which was reprinted in Volume V of the *Collected Papers of Charles Sanders Peirce*, edited by Charles Hartshorne and Paul Weiss (Cambridge, Mass.: Harvard University Press, 1934).

fice" can be cited to defend the "foundations." The two-tier model of the traditional theory appears to be too simple to account for the complexity of actual verification procedures.

At this point one might wonder how sense experience is related to knowledge at all. Popper in his well-known falsifiability thesis which is presented in the seventh selection asserts that sensations do not provide a basis from which theories can be confirmed or verified. Theories cannot be confirmed by inferring them from statements about direct experience. Theories are guesses or conjectures intended to explain observable facts. They are tested not by being inferred from some nonexistent foundation but by setting up experimental situations in which an attempt is made to refute or falsify them. The most that experience can do is show that a theory is wrong, but not provide reasons for thinking it is right.

Quine, on the other hand, argues that sense experience in some way provides evidence for theories. In addition, he insists that certain other principles play an important role in what we accept. In forming our beliefs we try to attain coherence and consistency; but often we confront a recalcitrant experience which forces us to revise the system. For example, suppose I thought that unicorns do not exist, but now I think I see one. I can surrender my former belief; or instead I can condemn my present perception as an hallucination; or with less plausibility, I can raise doubts about the laws of logic. A recalcitrant experience, says Quine, does not settle the issue of what to do, but leaves it to our decision. In making a choice, we are guided both by a conservative principle—"our natural tendency to disturb the total system as little as possible"—and also by a potentially revolutionary principle—"the quest for simplicity." Sense experience for Quine is not so much a foundation of knowledge as it is a stimulus provoking us to institute revisions in our system of beliefs.

We noted earlier that the theory that knowledge must have foundations was often based upon an infinite regress argument. Unless there is a stopping place in the order of reasons and evidence, we can never know anything. Nelson Goodman (in the tenth selection) accepts something like the traditional argument: "Now clearly we cannot suppose that statements derive their credibility from other statements without ever bringing this string of statements to earth. Credibility may be transmitted from one statement to another through deductive or probability connections; but credibility does not spring from these connections by spontaneous generation. Somewhere along the line some statements, whether atomic sense reports or the entire system or something in between, must have initial credibility." According to traditional argument, derived knowledge presupposes intuitive knowledge. According to Goodman's version, statements with derived credibility presuppose statements with non-derived or "initial" credibility. Although initial credibility does not imply certainty, Goodman's view is not far from the traditional theory since it implies that all credible beliefs have a foundation in beliefs initially credible. Without such a doctrine of initial credibility, it is not clear how we can have knowledge or justified belief about the world based on sense experience. If sense experience merely causes us to revise our system of beliefs, it would be a mystery how the revised beliefs can be justified, warranted, or counted as knowledge. But if our revisions are justified by being based on sense experience, experience or statements about it must then be the source of the justification; and Goodman's account is a plausible explanation of the origin, not of our beliefs, but of our justified beliefs.

In any case, the debate about the foundations of knowledge has not yet ended. The question still to be resolved is how sense experience contributes to knowledge. The issue of the basis of *a priori* knowledge is still being vigorously discussed. The selections that follow are not records of something that is over and done with but represent a continuing dialogue over issues that are still very much alive.

part one

WHAT IS
KNOWLEDGE?

C. I. LEWIS

Knowledge as True Justified Belief

It is true of "knowledge" also, as it is of "action," that the term is used sometimes in a narrower, sometimes in a wider sense. Examples of knowing are typically chosen from those which answer to the narrower meaning, although limitation of the term to such as these would be incompatible with the practical importance assigned to knowledge, and with the common assumption that humans are engaged in knowing, of one sort or another, through most of their waking hours. To an extent not commonly remarked, the demands we make of what is to be called knowledge, when compared with the things we say unhesitatingly that we know, could easily lead to the conclusion that most attributions of knowledge are made by a kind of fiction.

First, it is requisite that knowing be an assertive state of mind; it must intend, point to, or mean something other than what is discoverable in the mental state itself. Further, this believing attitude lays claim to truth: it submits itself to appraisal as correct or incorrect by reference to this something which it intends. Its status as knowledge is, by such intent, not determinable through examining the state of mind itself but only by the relation of it to something else. And again, no believing state is to be classed as knowledge unless it has some ground or reason. It must be distinguished not only from false belief but also from that which is groundless and from the

* From C. I. Lewis, *An Analysis of Knowledge and Valuation*, 1946. Reprinted by permission of The Open Court Publishing Co., La Salle, Ill.

merely fortunate hazard of assertion. Knowledge is belief which not only is true but also is justified in its believing attitude.

Whoever knows or claims to know must admit the pertinence of the challenge, "*How* do you know; what warrants you in believing?" And he must also find answer to the even more fundamental challenge, "What do you mean; what fact or state of affairs do you point to; and how will what you indicate disclose itself?" Implicitly he agrees that he should recede from his assertive attitude if either of these two challenges cannot be met. Yet if only such mental states as clearly include the answer to these questions should be accounted knowledge, then cognition, instead of being a pervasive phenomenon of human life, would be one which is highly exceptional. Particularly so if such answers should be required to be explicit and complete: in that case knowledge would probably be nonexistent.

Knowledge shades off, on the one side, into those active attitudes, induced by past experience, which are its counterpart in animal life and presumably represent the phenomenon from which genetically the human type of knowing has arisen. On the other, it merges into unconsidered response such as was originally accompanied by explicit consideration and judgment but has now become habitual and semi-automatic because it characteristically leads to satisfactory results. In such cases, the sense of what is meant is vague or indicated only by the active attitude itself; and any justifying ground is adumbrated rather than explicit. If a child ask us which is his right hand, we tell him without hesitation. But if he asks *why* is that his right hand—a demand to explicate the meaning of the statement—we are irritated, because we do not easily summon the correct answer. And if he should be distrustful enough to inquire what makes us think that this is his right hand, we should be outraged; injured in our *amour propre* of maturity, which is so comfortably assured of many things the ground of which escapes us at the moment. Almost one can say that the surer we are of what we know, the less clear we are as to precisely what we mean and just how we know it. Knowledge so characteristically consists of items we have comfortably filed away in their proper pigeonholes as finished business. Even in the best and clearest cases of knowledge, such as are likely to be put forward as examples, our sense of what is meant, and our sense of the basis of belief, will be incomplete. We can go a little way in explication of these, but to go further would become progressively more difficult.

The utmost that can be demanded is that one who is said truly to know should be able to provide such explication when the need of it is genuine, and after reflection, and up to a certain point—the point where we reach what is already understood or what may be taken for granted.

Yet if in the analysis of knowledge we characteristically substitute for the relatively vague and inexplicit believing attitude an ideal explanation of it, this procedure has its warrant. Knowledge is not a descriptive but a normative category: it claims correctness; mental states are classified as genuine knowing only on assumption of such correctness. Epistemology is not psychological description of such mental states, but is critique of their cognitive claim; the assessment of their veracity and validity, and the eliciting of those criteria by which such claim may be attested.

Knowledge, Error, and Probable Opinion

~~~~~~

The question as to what we mean by truth and falsehood, which we considered in the preceding chapter, is of much less interest than the question as to how we can know what is true and what is false. This question will occupy us in the present chapter. There can be no doubt that *some* of our beliefs are erroneous; thus we are led to inquire what certainty we can ever have that such and such a belief is not erroneous. In other words, can we ever *know* anything at all, or do we merely sometimes by good luck believe what is true? Before we can attack this question, we must, however, first decide what we mean by "knowing," and this question is not so easy as might be supposed.

At first sight we might imagine that knowledge could be defined as "true belief." When what we believe is true, it might be supposed that we had achieved a knowledge of what we believe. But this would not accord with the way in which the word is commonly used. To take a very trivial instance: If a man believes that the late Prime Minister's last name began with a B, he believes what is true, since the late Prime Minister was Sir Henry Campbell Bannerman. But if he believes that Mr. Balfour was the late Prime Minister, he will still believe that the late Prime Minister's last name began with a B, yet this belief, though true, would not be thought to constitute knowledge. If a newspaper, by an intelligent anticipation, an-

* This selection consists of chapter 13 of *The Problems of Philosophy* by Bertrand Russell. It is reprinted with the permission of the Oxford University Press.

nounces the result of a battle before any telegram giving the result has been received, it may by good fortune announce what afterwards turns out to be the right result, and it may produce belief in some of its less experienced readers. But in spite of the truth of their belief, they cannot be said to have knowledge. Thus it is clear that a true belief is not knowledge when it is deduced from a false belief.

In like manner, a true belief cannot be called knowledge when it is deduced by a fallacious process of reasoning, even if the premisses from which it is deduced are true. If I know that all Greeks are men and that Socrates was a man, and I infer that Socrates was a Greek, I cannot be said to *know* that Socrates was a Greek, because, although my premisses and my conclusion are true, the conclusion does not follow from the premisses.

But are we to say that nothing is knowledge except what is validly deduced from true premisses? Obviously we cannot say this. Such a definition is at once too wide and too narrow. In the first place, it is too wide, because it is not enough that our premisses should be *true*, they must also be *known*. The man who believes that Mr. Balfour was the late Prime Minister may proceed to draw valid deductions from the true premiss that the late Prime Minister's name began with a B, but he cannot be said to *know* the conclusions reached by these deductions. Thus we shall have to amend our definition by saying that knowledge is what is validly deduced from *known* premisses. This, however, is a circular definition: it assumes that we already know what is meant by "known premisses." It can, therefore, at best define one sort of knowledge, the sort we call derivative, as opposed to intuitive knowledge. We may say: "*Derivative* knowledge is what is validly deduced from premisses known intuitively." In this statement there is no formal defect, but it leaves the definition of *intuitive* knowledge still to seek.

Leaving on one side, for the moment, the question of intuitive knowledge, let us consider the above suggested definition of derivative knowledge. The chief objection to it is that it unduly limits knowledge. It constantly happens that people entertain a true belief, which has grown up in them because of some piece of intuitive knowledge from which it is capable of being validly inferred, but from which it has not, as a matter of fact, been inferred by any logical process.

Take, for example, the beliefs produced by reading. If the newspapers announce the death of the King, we are fairly well justified in believing that the King is dead, since this is the sort of announcement which would not be made if it were false. And we are quite amply justified in believing that the newspaper asserts that the King is dead. But here the intuitive knowledge upon which our belief is based is knowledge of the existence of sense-data derived from looking at the print which gives the news. This knowledge scarcely rises into consciousness, except in a person who cannot read easily. A child may be aware of the shapes of the letters, and pass gradually and painfully to a realization of their meaning. But anybody accustomed to reading passes at once to what the letters mean, and is not aware, except on reflection, that he has derived this knowledge from the sense-data called seeing the printed letters. Thus although a valid inference from the letters to their meaning is possible, and *could* be performed by the reader, it is not in fact performed, since he does not in fact perform any operation which can be called logical inference. Yet it would be absurd to say that the reader does not *know* that the newspaper announces the King's death.

We must, therefore, admit as derivative knowledge whatever is the result of intuitive knowledge even if by mere association, provided there *is* a valid logical connexion, and the person in question could become aware of this connexion by reflection. There are in fact many ways, besides logical inference, by which we pass from one belief to another: the passage from the print to its meaning illustrates these ways. These ways may be called "psychological inference." We shall, then, admit such psychological inference as a means of obtaining derivative knowledge, provided there is a discoverable logical inference which runs parallel to the psychological inference. This renders our definition of derivative knowledge less precise than we could wish, since the word "discoverable" is vague: it does not tell us how much reflection may be needed in order to make the discovery. But in fact "knowledge" is not a precise conception: it merges into "probable opinion," as we shall see more fully in the course of the present chapter. A very precise definition, therefore, should not be sought, since any such definition must be more or less misleading.

The chief difficulty in regard to knowledge, however, does not arise over derivative knowledge, but over intuitive knowledge. So long as we are dealing with derivative knowledge, we have the test of intuitive knowledge to fall back upon. But in regard to intuitive beliefs, it is by no means easy to discover any criterion by which to distinguish some as true and others as erroneous. In this question it is scarcely possible to reach any very precise result: all our knowledge of truths is infected with *some* degree of doubt, and a theory which ignored this fact would be plainly wrong. Something may be done, however, to mitigate the difficulties of the question.

Our theory of truth, to begin with, supplies the possibility of distinguishing certain truths as *self-evident* in a sense which ensures infallibility. When a belief is true, we said, there is a corresponding fact, in which the several objects of the belief form a single complex. The belief is said to constitute *knowledge* of this fact, provided it fulfils those further somewhat vague conditions which we have been considering in the present chapter. But in regard to any fact, besides the knowledge constituted by belief, we may also have the kind of knowledge constituted by *perception* (taking this word in its widest possible sense). For example, if you know the hour of the sunset, you can at that hour know the fact that the sun is setting: this is knowledge of the fact by way of knowledge of *truths;* but you can also, if the weather is fine, look to the west and actually see the setting sun: you then know the same fact by the way of knowledge of *things.*

Thus in regard to any complex fact, there are, theoretically, two ways in which it may be known: (1) by means of a judgement, in which its several parts are judged to be related as they are in fact related; (2) by means of *acquaintance* with the complex fact itself, which may (in a large sense) be called perception, though it is by no means confined to objects of the senses. Now it will be observed that the second way of knowing a complex fact, the way of acquaintance, is only possible when there really is such a fact, while the first way, like all judgement, is liable to error. The second way gives us the complex whole, and is therefore only possible when its parts do actually have that relation which makes them combine to form such a complex. The first way, on the contrary, gives us the parts and the relation severally, and demands only the reality of the parts and the relation: the relation may not relate those parts in that way, and yet the judgement may occur.

It will be remembered that at the end of Chapter XI we suggested that there might be two kinds of self-evidence, one giving an absolute guarantee of truth, the other only a partial guarantee. These two kinds can now be distinguished.

We may say that a truth is self-evident, in the first and most absolute sense, when we have acquaintance with the fact which corresponds to the truth. When Othello believes that Desdemona loves Cassio, the corresponding fact, if his belief were true, would be "Desdemona's love for Cassio." This would be a fact with which no one could have acquaintance except Desdemona; hence in the sense of self-evidence that we are considering, the truth that Desdemona loves Cassio (if it were a truth) could only be self-evident to Desdemona. All mental facts, and all facts concerning sense data, have this same privacy: there is only one person to whom they can be self-evident in our present sense, since there is only one person who can be acquainted with the mental things or the sense data concerned. Thus no fact about any particular existing thing can be self-evident to more than one person. On the other hand, facts about universals do not have this privacy. Many minds may be acquainted with the same universals; hence a relation between universals may be known by acquaintance to many different people. In all cases where we know by acquaintance a complex fact consisting of certain terms in a certain relation, we say that the truth that these terms are so related has the first or absolute kind of self-evidence, and in these cases the judgement that the terms are so related *must* be true. Thus this sort of self-evidence is an absolute guarantee of truth.

But although this sort of self-evidence is an absolute guarantee of truth, it does not enable us to be *absolutely* certain, in the case of any given judgement, that the judgement in question is true. Suppose we first perceive the sun shining, which is a complex fact, and thence proceed to make the judgement "the sun is shining." In passing from the perception to the judgement, it is necessary to analyse the given complex fact: we have to separate out "the sun" and "shining" as constituents of the fact. In this process it is possible to commit an error; hence even where a *fact* has the first or absolute kind of self-evidence, a judgment believed to correspond to the fact is not absolutely infallible, because it may not really correspond to the fact. But if it does correspond (in the sense explained in the preceding chapter), then it *must* be true.

The second sort of self-evidence will be that which belongs to judgements in the first instance, and is not derived from direct perception of a fact as a single complex whole. This second kind of self-evidence will have degrees, from the very highest degree down to a bare inclination in favour of the belief. Take, for example, the case of a horse trotting away from us along a hard road. At first our certainty that we hear the hoofs is complete; gradually, if we listen intently, there comes a moment when we think perhaps it was imagination or the blind upstairs or our own heartbeats; at last we become doubtful whether there was any noise at all; then we *think* we no longer hear anything, and at last we *know* we no longer hear anything. In this process, there is a continual gradation of self-evidence, from the highest degree to the least, not in the sense data themselves, but in the judgements based on them.

Or again: Suppose we are comparing two shades of colour, one blue and one green. We can be quite sure they are different shades of colour; but if the green colour is gradually altered to be more and more like the blue, becoming first a blue-green, then a greeny-blue, then blue, there will come a moment when we are doubtful whether we can see any difference, and then a moment when we know that we cannot see any difference. The same thing happens in tuning a musical instrument, or in any other case where there is a continuous gradation. Thus self-evidence of this sort is a matter of degree; and it seems plain that the higher degrees are more to be trusted than the lower degrees.

In derivative knowledge our ultimate premisses must have some degree of self-evidence, and so must their connexion with the conclusions deduced from them. Take for example a piece of reasoning in geometry. It is not enough that the axioms from which we start should be self-evident: it is necessary also that, at each step in the reasoning, the connexion of premiss and conclusion should be self-evident. In difficult reasoning, this connexion has often only a very small degree of self-evidence; hence errors of reasoning are not improbable where the difficulty is great.

From what has been said it is evident that, both as regards intuitive knowledge and as regards derivative knowledge, if we assume that intuitive knowledge is trustworthy in proportion to the degree of its self-evidence, there will be a gradation in trustworthiness, from the existence of noteworthy sense-data and the simpler truths of logic and arithmetic, which may be taken as quite certain, down to judgements which seem only just more probable than their opposites. What we firmly believe, if it is true, is called *knowledge*, provided it is either intuitive or inferred (logically or psychologically) from intuitive knowledge from which it follows logically. What we firmly believe, if it is not true, is called *error*. What we firmly believe, if it is neither knowledge nor error, and also what we believe hesitatingly, because it is, or is derived from, something which has not the highest degree of self-evidence, may be called *probable opinion*. Thus the greater part of what would commonly pass as knowledge is more or less probable opinion.

In regard to probable opinion, we can derive great assistance from *coherence*, which we rejected as the *definition* of truth, but may often use as a *criterion*. A body of individually probable opinions, if they are mutually coherent, become more probable than any one of them would be individually. It is in this way that many scientific hypotheses acquire their probability. They fit into a coherent system of probable opinions, and thus become more probable than they would be in isolation. The same thing applies to general philosophical hypotheses. Often in a single case such hypotheses may seem highly doubtful, while yet, when we consider the order and coherence which they introduce into a mass of probable opinion, they become pretty nearly certain. This applies, in particular, to such matters as the distinction between dreams and waking life. If our dreams, night after night, were as coherent one with another as our days, we should hardly know whether to believe the dreams or the waking life. As it is, the test of coherence condemns the dreams and confirms the waking life. But this test, though it increases probability where it is successful, never gives absolute certainty, unless there is certainty already at some point in the coherent system. Thus the mere organization of probable opinion will never, by itself, transform it into indubitable knowledge.

part two

THE FOUNDATIONS OF KNOWLEDGE: ALTERNATIVE ACCOUNTS IN THE HISTORY OF PHILOSOPHY

RENÉ DESCARTES

A Rationalist Approach
to the Foundations of
Knowledge

(1) INTUITION AND DEDUCTION

We shall here take note of all those mental operations by which we are able, wholly without fear of illusion, to arrive at the knowledge of things. Now I admit only two, namely, intuition and deduction.

By *intuition* I understand, not the fluctuating testimony of the senses, nor the misleading judgment that proceeds from the blundering constructions of imagination, but the conception which an unclouded and attentive mind gives us so readily and distinctly that we are wholly freed from doubt about that which we understand. Or, what comes to the same thing, *intuition* is the undoubting conception of an unclouded and attentive mind, and springs from the light of reason alone; it is more certain than deduction itself, in that it is simpler, though deduction, as we have noted above, cannot by us be erroneously conducted. Thus each individual can mentally have intuition of the fact that he exists, and that he thinks; that the triangle is bounded by three lines only, the sphere by a single superficies, and so on. Facts of such a kind are far more numerous than many people think, disdaining as they do to direct their attention upon such simple matters.

---

* Part (1) of this selection is from Descartes' *Rules for the Direction of the Mind*. Parts (2) and (3) consist of the first two meditations from Descartes' *Meditations on First Philosophy*. The translation used is from *The Philosophical Works of Descartes* by E. S. Haldane and G. R. T. Ross, 1931. Reprinted by permission of the Cambridge University Press.

But in case anyone may be put out by this new use of the term intuition and of other terms which in the following pages I am similarly compelled to dissever from their current meaning, I here make the general announcement that I pay no attention to the way in which particular terms have of late been employed in the schools, because it would have been difficult to employ the same terminology while my theory was wholly different. All that I take note of is the meaning of the Latin of each word, when, in cases where an appropriate term is lacking, I wish to transfer to the vocabulary that expresses my own meaning those that I deem most suitable.

This evidence and certitude, however, which belongs to intuition, is required not only in the enunciation of propositions, but also in discursive reasoning of whatever sort. For example consider this consequence: two and two amount to the same as three and one. Now we need to see intuitively not only that two and two make four, and that likewise three and one make four, but further that the third of the above statements is a necessary conclusion from these two.

Hence now we are in a position to raise the question as to why we have, besides intuition, given this supplementary method of knowing, namely, knowing by *deduction*, by which we understand all necessary inference from other facts that are known with certainty. This, however, we could not avoid, because many things are known with certainty, though not by themselves evident, but only deduced from true and known principles by the continuous and uninterrupted action of a mind that has a clear vision of each step in the process. It is in a similar way that we know that the last link in a long chain is connected with the first, even though we do not take in by means of one and the same act of vision all the intermediate links on which that connection depends, but only remember that we have taken them successively under review and that each single one is united to its neighbour, from the first even to the last. Hence we distinguish this mental intuition from deduction by the fact that into the conception of the latter there enters a certain movement or succession, into that of the former there does not. Further deduction does not require an immediately presented evidence such as intuition possesses; its certitude is rather conferred upon it in some way by memory. The upshot of the matter is that it is possible to say that those propositions indeed which are immediately deduced from first principles are known now by intuition, now by deduction, that is, in a way that differs according to our point of view. But the first principles themselves are given by intuition alone, while, on the contrary, the remote conclusions are furnished only by deduction.

These two methods are the most certain routes to knowledge, and the mind should admit no others.

(2) THE SPHERE OF THE DOUBTFUL

It is now some years since I detected how many were the false beliefs that I had from my earliest youth admitted as true, and how doubtful was everything I had since constructed on this basis; and from that time I was convinced that I must once for all seriously undertake to rid myself of all the opinions which I had formerly accepted, and commence to build anew from the foundation, if I wanted to establish any firm and permanent structure in the sciences. But as this enterprise appeared to be a very great one, I waited until I had attained an age so mature that I could not hope that at any later date I should be better fitted to execute my design. This reason caused me to delay so long that I should feel that I was doing wrong were I to occupy in deliberation the time that yet remains to me for action. Today, then, since very opportunely for the plan I have in view I have delivered my mind from every care [and am happily agitated by no passions] and since I have procured for myself an assured leisure in a peaceable retirement, I shall at last seriously and freely address myself to the general upheaval of all my former opinions.

Now for this object it is not necessary that I should show that all of these are false—I shall perhaps never arrive at this end. But inasmuch as reason already persuades me that I ought no less carefully to withhold my assent from matters which are not entirely certain and indubitable than from those which appear to me manifestly to be false, if I am able to find in each one some reason to doubt, this will suffice to justify my rejecting the whole. And for that end it will not be requisite that I should examine each in particular, which would be an endless undertaking; for owing to the fact that the destruction of the foundations of necessity brings with it the downfall of the rest of the edifice, I shall only in the first place attack those principles upon which all my former opinions rested.

All that up to the present time I have accepted as most true and certain I have learned either from the senses or through the senses; but it is sometimes proved to me that these senses are deceptive, and it is wiser not to trust entirely to any thing by which we have once been deceived.

But it may be that although the senses sometimes deceive us concerning things which are hardly perceptible, or very far away, there are yet many others to be met with as to which we cannot reasonably have any doubt, although we recognise them by their means. For example, there is the fact that I am here, seated by the fire, attired in a dressing gown, having this paper in my hands and other similar matters. And how could I deny that these hands and this body are mine, were it not perhaps that I compare myself to certain persons, devoid of sense, whose cerebella are so troubled and clouded by the violent vapours of black bile, that they constantly assure us that they think they are kings when they are really quite poor, or that they are clothed in purple when they are really without covering, or who imagine that they have an earthenware head or are nothing but pumpkins or are made of glass. But they are mad, and I should not be any the less insane were I to follow examples so extravagant.

At the same time I must remember that I am a man, and that consequently I am in the habit of sleeping, and in my dreams representing to myself the same things or sometimes even less probable things, than do those who are insane in their waking moments. How often has it happened to me that in the night I dreamt that I found myself in this particular place, that I was dressed and seated near the fire, whilst in reality I was lying undressed in bed! At this moment it does indeed seem to me that it is with eyes awake that I am looking at this paper; that this head which I move is not asleep, that it is deliberately and of set purpose that I extend my hand and perceive it; what happens in sleep does not appear so clear nor so distinct as does all this. But in thinking over this I remind myself that on many occasions I have in sleep been deceived by similar illusions, and in dwelling carefully on this reflection I see so manifestly that there are no certain indications by which we may clearly distinguish wakefulness from sleep that I am lost in astonishment. And my astonishment is such that it is almost capable of persuading me that I now dream.

Now let us assume that we are asleep and that all these particulars, for example, that we open our eyes, shake our head, extend our hands, and so on, are but false delusions; and let us reflect that possibly neither our hands nor our whole body are such as they appear to us to be. At the same time we must at least confess that the things which are represented to us in sleep are like painted representations which can only have been formed as the counterparts of something real and true, and that in this way those general things at least, that is, eyes, a head, hands, and a whole body, are not imaginary things, but things really existent. For, as a matter of fact, painters, even when they study with the greatest skill to represent sirens and satyrs by forms the most strange and extraordinary, cannot give them natures which are entirely new, but merely make a certain medley of the members of different animals; or if their imagination is extravagant enough to invent something so novel that nothing similar has ever before been seen, and that then their work represents a thing purely fictitious and absolutely false, it is certain all the same that the colours of which this is composed are necessarily real. And for the same reason, although these general things, to wit, [a body], eyes, a head, hands, and such like, may be imaginary, we are bound at the same time to confess that there are at least some other objects yet more simple and more universal, which are real and true; and of these just in the same way as with certain real colours, all these images of things which dwell in our thoughts, whether true and real or false and fantastic, are formed.

To such a class of things pertains corporeal nature in general, and its extension, the figure of extended things, their quantity or magnitude and number, as also the place in which they are, the time which measures their duration, and so on.

That is possibly why our reasoning is not unjust when we conclude from this that Physics, Astronomy, Medicine and all other sciences which have as their end the consideration of composite things, are very dubious and uncertain; but that Arithmetic, Geometry and other sciences of that kind which only treat of things that are very simple and very general, without taking great trouble to ascertain whether they are actually existent or not, contain some measure of certainty and an element of the indubitable. For whether I am awake or asleep, two and three together always form five, and the square can never have more than four sides, and it does not seem possible that truths so clear and apparent can be suspected of any falsity [or uncertainty].

Nevertheless I have long had fixed in my mind the belief that an all-powerful God existed by whom I have been created such as I am. But how do I know that He has not brought it to pass that there is no earth, no heaven, no extended body, no magnitude, no place, and that nevertheless [I possess the perceptions of all these things and that] they seem to me to exist just exactly as I now see them? And, besides, as I sometimes imagine that others deceive themselves in the things which they think they know best, how do I know that I am not deceived every time that I add two and three, or count the sides of a square, or judge of things yet simpler, if anything simpler can be imagined? But possibly God has not desired that I should be thus deceived, for He is said to be supremely good. If, however, it is contrary to His goodness to have made me such that I constantly deceive myself, it would also appear to be contrary to His goodness to permit me to be sometimes deceived, and nevertheless I cannot doubt that He does permit this.

There may indeed be those who would prefer to deny the existence of a God so powerful, rather than believe that all other things are uncertain. But let us not oppose them for the present, and grant that all that is here said of a God is a fable; nevertheless in whatever way they suppose that I have arrived at the state of being that I have reached—whether they attribute it to fate or to accident, or make out that it is by a continual succession of antecedents, or by some other method—since to err and deceive oneself is a defect, it is clear that the greater will be the probability of my being so imperfect as to deceive myself ever, as is the Author to whom they assign my origin the less powerful. To these reasons I have certainly nothing to reply, but at the end I feel constrained to confess that there is nothing in all that I formerly believed to be true, of which I cannot in some measure doubt, and that not merely through want of thought or through levity, but for reasons which are very powerful and maturely considered; so that henceforth I ought not the less carefully to refrain from giving credence to these opinions than to that which is manifestly false, if I desire to arrive at any certainty [in the sciences].

But it is not sufficient to have made these remarks, we must also be careful to keep them in mind. For these ancient and commonly held opinions still revert frequently to my mind, long and familiar custom having given them the right to occupy my mind against my inclination and rendered them almost masters of my belief; nor will I ever lose the habit of deferring to them or of placing my confidence in them, so long as I consider them as they really are, that is, opinions in some measure doubtful, as I have just shown, and at the same time highly probable, so that there is much more reason to believe in than to deny them. That is why I consider that I shall not be acting amiss, if, taking of set purpose a contrary belief, I allow myself to be deceived, and for a certain time pretend that all these opinions are entirely false and imaginary, until at last, having thus balanced my former prejudices with my latter [so that they cannot divert my opinions more to one side than to the other], my judgment will no longer be dominated by bad usage or turned away from the right knowledge of the truth. For I am assured that there can be neither peril nor error in this course, and that I cannot at present yield too much to distrust, since I am not considering the question of action, but only of knowledge.

I shall then suppose, not that God who is supremely good and the fountain of truth, but some evil genius not less powerful than deceitful, has employed his whole energies in deceiving me; I shall consider that the heavens, the earth, colours, figures, sound, and all other external things are nought but the illusions and dreams of which this genius has availed himself in order to lay traps for my credulity; I shall consider myself as having no hands, no eyes, no flesh, no blood, nor any senses, yet falsely believing myself to possess all these things; I shall remain obstinately attached to this idea, and if by this means it is not in my power to arrive at the knowledge of any truth, I may at least do what is in my power [i.e., suspend my judgment], and with firm purpose avoid giving credence to any false thing, or being imposed upon by this arch deceiver, however powerful and deceptive he may be. But this task is a laborious one, and insensibly a certain lassitude leads me into the course of my ordinary life. And just as a captive who in sleep enjoys an imaginary liberty, when he begins to suspect that his liberty is but a dream, fears to awaken, and conspires with these agreeable illusions that the deception may be prolonged, so insensibly of my own accord I fall back into my former opinions, and I dread awakening from this slumber, lest the laborious wakefulness which would follow the tranquillity of this repose should have to be spent not in daylight, but in the excessive darkness of the difficulties which have just been discussed.

[Editor's note: In his reply to the *Seventh Set of Objections* Descartes provides the following justification of the method of doubt which he had begun to apply in the first meditation. "Here I shall make use of a very homely example for the purpose of explaining to him the rationale of my procedure, in order that in future he may not misunderstand it or dare to pretend that he does not understand it. Supposing he had a basket of apples and, fearing that some of them were rotten, wanted to take those out lest they might make the rest go wrong, how could he do that? Would he not first turn the whole of the apples out of the basket and look them over one by one, and then having selected those which he saw not to be rotten, place them again in the basket and leave out the others? It is therefore just in the same way that those who have never rightly philosophized have in their mind a variety of opinions some of which they justly fear not to be true, seeing that it was in their earliest years that they began to amass those beliefs. They then try to separate the false from the true lest the presence of the former should produce a general uncertainty about all. Now there is no better way of doing this than to reject all at once together as uncertain or false, and then having inspected each singly and in order, to reinstate only those which they know to be true and indubitable."]

(3) KNOWLEDGE OF MIND AND OF BODY

The Meditation of yesterday filled my mind with so many doubts that it is no longer in my power to forget them. And yet I do not see in what manner I can resolve them; and, just as if I had all of a sudden fallen into very deep water, I am so disconcerted that I can neither make certain of setting my feet on the bottom, nor can I swim and so support myself on the surface. I shall nevertheless make an effort and follow anew the same path as that on which I yesterday entered, that is, I shall proceed by setting aside all that in which the least doubt could be supposed to exist, just as if I had discovered that it was absolutely false; and I shall ever follow in this road until I have met with something which is certain, or at least, if I can do nothing else, until I have learned for certain that there is nothing in the world that is certain. Archimedes, in order that he might draw the terrestrial globe out of its place, and transport it elsewhere, demanded only that one point should be fixed and immoveable; in the same way I shall have the right to conceive high hopes if I am happy enough to discover one thing only which is certain and indubitable.

I suppose, then, that all the things that I see are false; I persuade myself that nothing has ever existed of all that my fallacious memory represents to me. I consider that I possess no senses; I imagine that body, figure, extension, movement and place are but the fictions of my mind. What, then, can be esteemed as true? Perhaps nothing at all, unless that there is nothing in the world that is certain.

But how can I know there is not something different from those things that I have just considered, of which one cannot have the slightest doubt? Is there not some God, or some other being by whatever name we call it, who puts these reflections into my mind? That is not necessary, for is it not possible that I am capable of producing them myself? I myself, am I not at least something? But I have already denied that I had senses and body. Yet I hesitate, for what follows from that? Am I so dependent on body and senses that I cannot exist without these? But I was persuaded that there was nothing in all the world, that there was no heaven, no earth, that there were no minds, nor any bodies: was I not then likewise persuaded that I did not exist? Not at all; of a surety I myself did exist since I persuaded myself of something [or merely because I thought of something]. But there is some deceiver or other, very powerful and very cunning, who ever employs his ingenuity in deceiving me. Then without doubt I exist also if he deceives me, and let him deceive me as much as he will, he can never cause me to be nothing so long as I think that I am something. So that after having reflected well and carefully examined all things, we must come to the definite conclusion that this proposition: I am, I exist, is necessarily true each time that I pronounce it, or that I mentally conceive it.

But I do not yet know clearly enough what I am, I who am certain that I am; and hence I must be careful to see that I do not imprudently take some other object in place of myself, and thus that I do not go astray in respect of this knowledge that I hold to be the most certain and most evident of all that I have formerly learned. That is why I shall now consider anew what I believed myself to be before I embarked upon these last reflections; and of my former opinions I shall withdraw all that might even in a small degree be invalidated by the reasons which I have just brought forward, in order that there may be nothing at all left beyond what is absolutely certain and indubitable.

What then did I formerly believe myself to be? Undoubtedly I believed myself to be a man. But what is a man? Shall I say a reasonable animal? Certainly not; for then I should have to inquire what an animal is, and what is reasonable; and thus from a single question I should insensibly fall into an infinitude of others more difficult; and I should not wish to waste the little time and leisure remaining to me in trying to unravel subtleties like these. But I shall rather stop here to consider the thoughts which of themselves spring up in my mind, and which were not inspired by anything beyond my own nature alone when I applied myself to the consideration of my being. In the first place, then, I considered myself as having a face, hands, arms, and all that system of members composed of bones and flesh as seen in a corpse which I designated by the name of body. In addition to this I considered that I was nourished, that I walked, that I felt, and that I thought, and I referred all these actions to the soul: but I did not stop to consider what the soul was, or if I did stop, I imagined that it was something extremely rare and subtle like a wind, a flame, or an ether, which was spread throughout my grosser parts. As to body I had no manner of doubt about its nature, but thought I had a very clear knowledge of it; and if I had desired to explain it according to the notions that I had then formed of it, I should have described it thus: By the body I understand all that which can be defined by a certain figure: something which can be confined in a certain place, and which can fill a given space in such a way that every other body will be excluded from it; which can be perceived either by touch, or by sight, or by hearing, or by taste, or by smell: which can be moved in many ways not, in truth, by itself, but by something which is foreign to it, by which it is touched [and from which it receives impressions]: for to have the power of self-movement, as also of feeling or of thinking, I did not consider to appertain to the nature of body: on the contrary, I was rather astonished to find that faculties similar to them existed in some bodies.

But what am I, now that I suppose that there is a certain genius which is extremely powerful, and, if I may say so, malicious, who employs all his powers in deceiving me? Can I affirm that I possess the least of all those things which I have just said pertain to the nature of body? I pause to consider, I revolve all these things in my mind, and I find none of which I can say that it pertains to me. It would be tedious to stop to enumerate them. Let us pass to the attributes of soul and see if there is any one which is in me? What of nutrition or walking [the first mentioned]? But if it is so that I have no body it is also true that I can neither walk nor take nourishment. Another attribute is sensation. But one cannot feel without body, and besides I have thought I perceived many things during sleep that I recognised in my waking moments as not having been experienced at all. What of thinking? I find here that thought is an attribute that belongs to me; it alone cannot be separated from me. I am, I exist, that is certain. But how often? Just when I think; for it might possibly be the case if I ceased entirely to think, that I should likewise cease altogether to exist. I do not now admit anything which is not necessarily true: to speak accurately I am not more than a thing which thinks, that is to say a mind or a soul, or an understanding, or a reason, which are terms whose significance was formerly unknown to me. I am, however, a real thing and really exist; but what thing? I have answered: a thing which thinks.

And what more? I shall exercise my imagination [in order to see if I am not something more]. I am not a collection of members which we call the human body: I am not a subtle air distributed through these members, I am not a wind, a fire, a vapour, a breath, nor anything at all which I can imagine or conceive; because I have assumed that all these were nothing. Without changing that supposition I find that I only leave myself certain of the fact that I am somewhat. But perhaps it is true that these same things which I supposed were nonexistent because they are unknown to me, are really not different from the self which I know. I am not sure about this, I shall not dispute about it now; I can only give judgment on things that are known to me. I know that I exist, and I inquire what I am, I whom I know to exist. But it is very certain that the knowledge of my existence taken in its precise significance does not depend on things whose existence is not yet known to me; consequently it does not depend on those which I can feign in imagination. And indeed the very term *feign* in imagination proves to me my error, for I really do this if I imagine myself a something, since to imagine is nothing else than to contemplate the figure or image of a corporeal thing. But I already know for certain that I am, and that it may be that all these images, and, speaking generally, all things that relate to the nature of body are nothing but dreams [and chimeras]. For this reason I see clearly that I have as little reason to say, "I shall stimulate my imagination in order to know more distinctly what I am," than if I were to say, "I am now awake, and I perceive somewhat that is real and true: but because I do not yet perceive it distinctly enough, I shall go to sleep of express purpose, so that my dreams may represent the perception with greatest truth and evidence." And, thus, I know for certain that nothing of all that I can understand by means of my imagination belongs to this knowledge which I have of myself, and that it is necessary to recall the mind from this mode of thought with the utmost diligence in order that it may be able to know its own nature with perfect distinctness.

But what then am I? A thing which thinks. What is a thing which thinks? It is a thing which doubts, understands, [conceives], affirms, denies, wills, refuses, which also imagines and feels.

Certainly it is no small matter if all these things pertain to my nature. But why should they not so pertain? Am I not that being who now doubts nearly everything, who nevertheless understands certain things, who affirms that one only is true, who denies all the others, who desires to know more, is averse from being deceived, who imagines many things, sometimes indeed despite his will, and who perceives many likewise, as by the intervention of the bodily organs? Is there nothing in all this which is as true as it is certain that I exist, even though I should always sleep and though he who has given me being employed all his ingenuity in deceiving me? Is there likewise any one of these attributes which can be distinguished from my thought, or which might be said to be separated from myself? For it is so evident of itself that it is I who doubts, who understands, and who desires, that there is no reason here to add anything to explain it. And I have certainly the power of imagining likewise; for although it may happen (as I formerly supposed) that none of the things which I imagine are true, nevertheless this power of imagining does not cease to be really in use, and it forms part of my thought. Finally, I am the same who feels, that is to say, who perceives certain things, as by the organs of sense, since in truth I see light, I hear noise, I feel heat. But it will be said that these phenomena are false and that I am dreaming. Let it be so; still it is at least quite certain that it seems to me that I see light, that I hear noise and that I feel heat. That cannot be false; properly speaking it is what is in me called feeling; and used in this precise sense that is no other thing than thinking.

From this time I begin to know what I am with a little more clearness and distinction than before; but nevertheless it still seems to me, and I cannot prevent myself from thinking, that corporeal things, whose images are framed by thought, which are tested by the senses, are much more distinctly known than that obscure part of me which does not come under the imagination. Although really it is very strange to say that I know and understand more distinctly these things whose existence seems to me dubious, which are unknown to me, and which do not belong to me, than others of the truth of which I am convinced, which are known to me and which pertain to my real nature, in a word, than myself. But I see clearly how the case stands: my mind loves to wander, and cannot yet suffer itself to be retained within the just limits of truth. Very good, let us once more give it the freest rein, so that, when afterwards we seize the proper occasion for pulling up, it may the more easily be regulated and controlled.

Let us begin by considering the commonest matters, those which we believe to be the most distinctly comprehended, to wit, the bodies which we touch and see; not indeed bodies in general, for these general ideas are usually a little more confused, but let us consider one body in particular. Let us take, for example, this piece of wax: it has been taken quite freshly from the hive, and it has not yet lost the sweetness of the honey which it contains; it still retains somewhat of the odour of the flowers from which it has been culled; its colour, its figure, its size are apparent; it is hard, cold, easily handled, and if you strike it with the finger, it will emit a sound. Finally all the things which are requisite to cause us distinctly to recognise a body, are met with in it. But notice that while I speak and approach the fire what remained of the taste is exhaled, the smell evaporates, the colour alters, the figure is destroyed, the size increases, it becomes liquid, it heats, scarcely can one handle it, and when one strikes it, no sound is emitted. Does the same wax remain after this change? We must confess that it remains; none would judge otherwise. What then did I know so distinctly in this piece of wax? It could certainly be nothing of all that the senses brought to my notice, since all these things which fall under taste, smell, sight, touch, and hearing, are found to be changed, and yet the same wax remains.

Perhaps it was what I now think, namely, that this wax was not that sweetness of honey, nor that agreeable scent of flowers, nor that particular whiteness, nor that figure, nor that sound, but simply a body which a little while before appeared to me as perceptible under these forms, and which is now perceptible under others. But what, precisely, is it that I imagine when I form such conceptions? Let us attentively consider this, and, abstracting from all that does not belong to the wax, let us see what remains. Certainly nothing remains excepting a certain extended thing which is flexible and movable. But what is the meaning of flexible and movable? Is it not that I imagine that this piece of wax being round is capable of becoming square and of passing from a square to a triangular figure? No, certainly it is not that, since I imagine it admits of an infinitude of similar changes, and I nevertheless do not know how to compass the infinitude by my imagination, and consequently this conception which I have of the wax is not brought about by the faculty of imagination. What now is this extension? Is it not also unknown? For it becomes greater when the wax is melted, greater when it is boiled, and greater still when the heat increases; and I should not conceive [clearly] according to truth what wax is, if I did not think that even this piece that we are considering is capable of receiving more variations in extension than I have ever imagined. We must then grant that I could not even understand through the imagination what this piece of wax is, and that it is my mind alone which perceives it. I say this piece of wax in particular, for as to wax in general it is yet clearer. But what is this piece of wax which cannot be understood excepting by the [understanding or] mind? It is certainly the same that I see, touch, imagine, and finally it is the same which I have always believed it to be from the beginning. But what must particularly be observed is that its perception is neither an act of vision, nor of touch, nor of imagination, and has never been such although it may have appeared formerly to be so, but only an intuition of the mind, which may be imperfect and confused as it was formerly, or clear and distinct as it is at present, according as my attention is more or less directed to the elements which are found in it, and of which it is composed.

Yet in the meantime I am greatly astonished when I consider [the great feebleness of mind] and its proneness to fall [insensibly] into error; for although without giving expression to my thoughts I consider all this in my own mind, words often impede me and I am almost deceived by the terms of ordinary language. For we say that we see the same wax, if it is present, and not that we simply judge that it is the same from its having the same colour and figure. From this I should conclude that I knew the wax by means of vision and not simply by the intuition of the mind; unless by chance I remember that, when looking from a window and saying I see men who pass in the street, I really do not see them, but infer that what I see is men, just as I say that I see wax. And yet what do I see from the window but hats and coats which may cover automatic machines? Yet I judge these to be men. And similarly solely by the faculty of judgment which rests in my mind, I comprehend that which I believed I saw with my eyes.

A man who makes it his aim to raise his knowledge above the common should be ashamed to derive the occasion for doubting from the forms of speech invented by the vulgar; I prefer to pass on and consider whether I had a more evident and perfect conception of what the wax was when I first perceived it, and when I believed I knew it by means of the external senses or at least by the common sense as it is called, that is to say by the imaginative faculty, or whether my present conception is clearer now that I have most carefully examined what it is, and in what way it can be known. It would certainly be absurd to doubt as to this. For what was there in this first perception which was distinct? What was there which might not as well have been perceived by any of the animals? But when I distinguish the wax from its external forms, and when, just as if I had taken from it its vestments, I consider it quite naked, it is certain that although some error may still be found in my judgment, I can nevertheless not perceive it thus without a human mind.

But finally what shall I say of this mind, that is, of myself, for up to this point I do not admit in myself anything but mind? What then, I who seem to perceive this piece of wax so distinctly, do I not know myself, not only with much more truth and certainty, but also with much more distinctness and clearness? For if I judge that the wax is or exists from the fact that I see it, it certainly follows much more clearly that I am or that I exist myself from the fact that I see it. For it may be that what I see is not really wax, it may also be that I do not possess eyes with which to see anything; but it cannot be that when I see, or (for I no longer take account of the distinction) when I think I see, that I myself who think am nought. So if I judge that the wax exists from the fact that I touch it, the same thing will follow, to wit, that I am; and if I judge that my imagination, or some other cause, whatever it is, persuades me that the wax exists, I shall still conclude the same. And what I have here remarked of wax may be applied to all other things which are external to me [and which are met with outside of me]. And further, if the [notion or] perception of wax has seemed to me clearer and more distinct, not only after the sight or the touch, but also after many other causes have rendered it quite manifest to me, with how much more [evidence] and distinctness must it be said that I now know myself, since all the reasons which contribute to the knowledge of wax, or any other body whatever, are yet better proofs of the nature of my mind! And there are so many other things in the mind itself which may contribute to the elucidation of its nature, that those which depend on body such as these just mentioned, hardly merit being taken into account.

But finally here I am, having insensibly reverted to the point I desired, for, since it is now manifest to me that even bodies are not properly speaking known by the senses or by the faculty of imagination, but by the understanding only, and since they are not known from the fact that they are seen or touched, but only because they are understood, I see clearly that there is nothing which is easier for me to know than my mind. But because it is difficult to rid oneself so promptly of an opinion to which one was accustomed for so long, it will be well that I should halt a little at this point, so that by the length of my meditation I may more deeply imprint on my memory this new knowledge.

JOHN LOCKE

An Empiricist Approach to the Foundations of Knowledge

(1) THE ORIGIN OF IDEAS

Every man being conscious to himself that he thinks; and that which his mind is applied about whilst thinking being the *ideas* that are there, it is past doubt that men have in their minds several ideas, such as are those expressed by the words *whiteness, hardness, sweetness, thinking, motion, man, elephant, army, drunkenness,* and others: it is in the first place then to be inquired, *How he comes by them?*

I know it is a received doctrine, that men have native ideas, and original characters, stamped upon their minds in their very first being. This opinion I have at large examined already; and, I suppose what I have said in the foregoing Book will be much more easily admitted, when I have shown whence the understanding may get all the ideas it has; and by what ways and degrees they may come into the mind; for which I shall appeal to every one's own observation and experience.

Let us then suppose the mind to be, as we say, white paper, void of all characters, without any ideas: How comes it to be furnished? Whence comes it by that vast store which the busy and boundless fancy of man has painted on it with an almost endless variety?

* This selection is from Locke's *An Essay Concerning Human Understanding.* Part (1) is from Book II, Chaps. 1 and 2; part (2) is from Book II, Chap. 8; and part (3) is from Book IV, Chaps. 1, 2, and 11.

Whence has it all the *materials* of reason and knowledge? To this I answer, in one word, from *experience*. In that all our knowledge is founded; and from that it ultimately derives itself. Our observation employed either, about external sensible objects, or about the internal operations of our minds perceived and reflected on by ourselves, is that which supplies our understandings with all the *materials* of thinking. These two are the fountains of knowledge, from whence all the ideas we have, or can naturally have, do spring.

First, our Senses, conversant about particular sensible objects, do convey into the mind several distinct perceptions of things, according to those various ways wherein those objects do affect them. And thus we come by those *ideas* we have of *yellow, white, heat, cold, soft, hard, bitter, sweet,* and all those which we call sensible qualities; which when I say the senses convey into the mind, I mean, they from external objects convey into the mind what produces there those perceptions. This great source of most of the ideas we have, depending wholly upon our senses, and derived by them to the understanding, I call *sensation.*

Secondly, the other fountain from which experience furnisheth the understanding with ideas is, the perception of the operations of our own mind within us, as it is employed about the ideas it has got; which operations, when the soul comes to reflect on and consider, do furnish the understanding with another set of ideas, which could not be had from things without. And such are *perception, thinking, doubting, believing, reasoning, knowing, willing,* and all the different actings of our own minds; which we being conscious of, and observing in ourselves, do from these receive into our understandings as distinct ideas as we do from bodies affecting our senses. This source of ideas every man has wholly in himself; and though it be not sense, as having nothing to do with external objects, yet it is very like it, and might properly enough be called *internal sense.* But as I call the other Sensation, so I call this *reflection,* the ideas it affords being such only as the mind gets by reflecting on its own operations within itself. By reflection then, in the following part of this discourse, I would be understood to mean, that notice which the mind takes of its own operations, and the manner of them, by reason whereof there come to be ideas of these operations in the understanding. These two, I say, namely, external material things, as the objects of *sensation,* and the operations of our own minds within, as the objects of *reflection,* are to me the only originals from whence all our ideas take their beginnings. The term *operations* here I use in a large sense, as comprehending not barely the actions of the mind about its ideas, but some sort of passions arising sometimes from them, such as is the satisfaction or uneasiness arising from any thought.

The understanding seems to me not to have the least glimmering of any ideas which it doth not receive from one of these two. *External objects* furnish the mind with the ideas of sensible qualities, which are all those different perceptions they produce in us; and *the mind* furnishes the understanding with ideas of its own operations.

These, when we have taken a full survey of them, and their several modes, combinations, and relations, we shall find to contain all our whole stock of ideas; and that we have nothing in our minds which did not come in one of these two ways. Let any one examine his own thoughts, and thoroughly search into his understanding; and then let him tell me, whether all the original ideas he has there, are any other than of the objects of his senses, or of the operations of his mind, considered as objects of his reflection. And how great a mass of knowledge soever he imagines to be lodged there, he will, upon taking a strict view, see that he has not any idea in his mind but what one of these two have imprinted; though perhaps, with infinite variety compounded and enlarged by the understanding, as we shall see hereafter.

He that attentively considers the state of a child, at his first coming into the world, will have little reason to think him stored with plenty of ideas, that are to be the matter of his future knowledge. It is *by degrees* he comes to be furnished with them. And though the ideas of obvious and familiar qualities imprint themselves before the memory begins to keep a register of time or order, yet it is often so late before some unusual qualities come in the way, that there are few men that cannot recollect the beginning of their acquaintance with them. And if it were worth while, no doubt a child might be so ordered as to have but a very few, even of the ordinary ideas, till he were grown up to a man. But all that are born into the world, being surrounded with bodies that perpetually and diversely affect them, variety of ideas, whether care be taken of it or not, are imprinted on the minds of children. Light and colours are busy at hand everywhere, when the eye is but open; sounds and some tangible qualities fail not to solicit their proper senses, and force an entrance to the mind; but yet, I think, it will be granted easily, that if a child were kept in a place where he never saw any other but black and white till he were a man, he would have no more ideas of scarlet or green, than he that from his childhood never tasted an oyster, or a pine-apple, has of those particular relishes.

•   •   •   •   •   •   •   •   •   •   •   •   •

In time the mind comes to reflect on its own operations about the ideas got by sensation, and thereby stores itself with a new set of ideas, which I call ideas of reflection. These are the impressions that are made on our senses by outward objects that are extrinsical to the mind; and its own operations, proceeding from powers intrinsical and proper to itself, which, when reflected on by itself, become also objects of its contemplation—are, as I have said, the original of all knowledge. Thus the first capacity of human intellect is, that the mind is fitted to receive the impressions made on it; either through the senses by outward objects, or by its own operations when it reflects on them. This is the first step a man makes towards the discovery of anything, and the groundwork whereon to build all those notions which ever he shall have naturally in this world. All those sublime thoughts which tower above the clouds, and reach as high as heaven itself, take their rise and footing here: in all that great extent wherein the mind wanders, in those remote speculations it may seem to be elevated with, it stirs not one jot beyond those ideas which *sense* or *reflection* have offered for its contemplation.

In this part the understanding is merely passive; and whether or no it will have these beginnings, and as it were materials of knowledge, is not in its own power. For the objects of our senses do, many of them, obtrude their particular ideas upon our minds whether we will or not; and the operations of our minds will not let us be without, at least, some obscure notions of them. No man can be wholly ignorant of what he does when he thinks. These simple ideas, when offered to the mind, the understanding can no more refuse to have, nor alter when they are imprinted, nor blot them out and make new ones itself, than a mirror can refuse, alter, or obliterate the images or ideas which the objects set before it do therein produce. As the bodies that surround us do diversely affect our organs, the mind is forced to receive the impressions; and cannot avoid the perception of those ideas that are annexed to them.

The better to understand the nature, manner, and extent of our knowledge, one thing is carefully to be observed concerning the ideas we have; and that is, that some of them are *simple* and some *complex*.

Though the qualities that affect our senses are, in the things themselves, so united and blended, that there is no separation, no distance between them; yet it is plain, the ideas they produce in the mind enter by the senses simple and unmixed. For, though the sight and touch often take in from the same object, at the same time, different ideas; as a man sees at once motion and colour; the hand feels softness and warmth in the same piece of wax: yet the simple ideas thus united in the same subject, are as perfectly distinct as those that come in by different senses. The coldness and hardness which a man feels in a piece of ice being as distinct ideas in the mind as the smell and whiteness of a lily; or as the taste of sugar, and smell of a rose. And there is nothing can be plainer to a man than the clear and distinct perception he has of those simple ideas; which, being each in itself uncompounded, contains in it nothing but *one uniform appearance, or conception in the mind,* and is not distinguishable into different ideas.

These simple ideas, the materials of all our knowledge, are suggested and furnished to the mind only by those two ways above mentioned, namely, sensation and reflection. When the understanding is once stored with these simple ideas, it has the power to repeat, compare, and unite them, even to an almost infinite variety, and so can make at pleasure new complex ideas. But it is not in the power of the most exalted wit, or enlarged understanding, by any quickness or variety of thought, to *invent* or *frame* one new simple idea in the mind, not taken in by the ways before mentioned: nor can any force of the understanding *destroy* those that are there. The dominion of man, in this little world of his own understanding being much what the same as it is in the great world of visible things; wherein his power, however managed by art and skill, reaches no farther than to compound and divide the materials that are made to his hand; but can do nothing towards the making the least particle of new matter, or destroying one atom of what is already in being. The same inability will every one find in himself, who shall go about to fashion in his understanding one simple idea, not received in by his senses from external objects, or by reflection from the operations of his own mind about them. I would have any one try to fancy any taste which had never affected his palate; or frame the idea of a scent he had never smelt: and when he can do this, I will also conclude that a blind man hath ideas of colours, and a deaf man true distinct notions of sounds.

(2) PRIMARY AND SECONDARY QUALITIES

To discover the nature of our *ideas* the better, and to discourse of them intelligibly, it will be convenient to distinguish them *as they are ideas or perceptions in our minds;* and *as they are modifications of matter in the bodies that cause such perceptions in us:* that so we may not think (as perhaps usually is done) that they are exactly the images and resemblances of something inherent in the subject; most of those of sensation being in the mind no more the likeness of something existing without us, than the names that stand for them are the likeness of our ideas, which yet upon hearing they are apt to excite in us.

Whatsoever the mind perceives *in itself,* or is the immediate object of perception, thought, or understanding, that I call *idea;* and the power to produce any idea in our mind, I call *quality* of the subject wherein the power is. Thus a snowball having the power to produce in us the ideas of white, cold, and round, the power to produce those ideas in us, as they are in the snowball, I call qualities; and as they are sensations or perceptions in our understanding, I call them ideas; which *ideas,* if I speak of sometimes as in the things themselves, I would be understood to mean those qualities in the objects which produce them in us.

Qualities thus considered in bodies are,

First, such as are utterly inseparable from the body, in what state soever it be; and such as in all the alterations and changes it suffers, all the force can be used upon it, it constantly keeps; and such as sense constantly finds in every particle of matter which has bulk enough to be perceived; and the mind finds inseparable from every particle of matter, though less than to make itself singly be perceived by our senses: for example, Take a grain of wheat, divide it into two parts; each part has still solidity, extension, figure, and mobility:

divide it again, and it retains still the same qualities; and so divide it on, till the parts become insensible; they must retain still each of them all those qualities. For division (which is all that a mill, or pestle, or any other body, does upon another, in reducing it to insensible parts) can never take away either solidity, extension, figure, or mobility from any body, but only makes two or more distinct separate masses of matter, of that which was but one before; all which distinct masses, reckoned as so many distinct bodies, after division, make a certain number. These I call *original* or *primary qualities* of body, which I think we may observe to produce simple ideas in us, namely, solidity, extension, figure, motion or rest, and number.

Secondly, such qualities which in truth are nothing in the objects themselves but powers to produce various sensations in us by their primary qualities, that is, by the bulk, figure, texture, and motion of their insensible parts, as colours, sounds, tastes, and so forth. These I call *secondary qualities.* To these might be added a *third* sort, which are allowed to be barely powers; though they are as much real qualities in the subject as those which I, to comply with the common way of speaking, call qualities, but for distinction, secondary qualities. For the power in fire to produce a new colour, or consistency, in *wax* or *clay,* by its primary qualities, is as much a quality in fire, as the power it has to produce in *me* a new idea or sensation of warmth or burning, which I felt not before, by the same primary qualities, namely, the bulk, texture, and motion of its insensible parts.

The next thing to be considered is, how bodies produce ideas in us; and that is manifestly by impulse, the only way which we can conceive bodies to operate in.

If then external objects be not united to our minds when they produce ideas therein; and yet we perceive these *original* qualities in such of them as singly fall under our senses, it is evident that some motion must be thence continued by our nerves, or animal spirits, by some parts of our bodies, to the brains or the seat of sensation, there to produce in our minds the particular ideas we have of them. And since the extension, figure, number, and motion of bodies of an observable bigness, may be perceived at a distance by the sight, it is evident some singly imperceptible bodies must come from them to the eyes, and thereby convey to the brain some motion; which produces these ideas which we have of them in us.

After the same manner that the ideas of these original qualities are produced in us, we may conceive that the ideas of *secondary* qualities are also produced, namely, by the operation of insensible particles on our senses. For, it being manifest that there are bodies and good store of bodies, each whereof are so small, that we cannot by any of our senses discover either their bulk, figure, or motion, as is evident in the particles of the air and water, and others extremely smaller than those; perhaps as much smaller than the particles of air and water, as the particles of air and water are smaller than peas or hail-stones; let us suppose at present that the different motions and figures, bulk and number, of such particles, affecting the several organs of our senses, produce in us those different sensations which we have from the colours and smells of bodies; for example, that a violet, by the impulse of such insensible particles of matter, of peculiar figures and bulks, and in different degrees and modifications of their motions, causes the ideas of the blue colour, and sweet scent of that flower to be produced in our minds. It being no more impossible to conceive that God should annex such ideas to such motions, with which they have no similitude, than that he should annex the idea of pain to the motion of a piece of steel dividing our flesh, with which that idea hath no resemblance.

What I have said concerning colours and smells may be understood also of tastes and sounds, and other the like sensible qualities; which, whatever reality we by mistake attribute to them, are in truth nothing in the objects themselves, but powers to produce various sensations in us; and depend on those primary qualities, namely, bulk, figure, texture, and motion of parts as I have said.

From whence I think it easy to draw this observation, that the ideas of primary qualities of bodies are resemblances of them, and their patterns do really exist in the bodies themselves, but the ideas produced in us by these secondary qualities have no resemblance of them at all. There is nothing like our ideas, existing in the bodies themselves. They are, in the bodies we denominate from them, only a power to produce those sensations in us: and what is sweet, blue, or warm in idea, is but the certain bulk, figure, and motion of the insensible parts, in the bodies themselves, which we call so.

Flame is denominated hot and light; snow, white and cold; and manna, white and sweet, from the ideas they produce in us. Which qualities are commonly thought to be the same in those bodies that those ideas are in us, the one the perfect resemblance of the other, as they are in a mirror, and it would by most men be judged very extravagant if one should say otherwise. And yet he that will consider that the same fire that, at one distance produces in us the sensation of warmth, does, at a nearer approach, produce in us the far different sensation of pain, ought to bethink himself what reason he has to say—that this idea of warmth, which was produced in him by the fire, is *actually in the fire*; and his idea of pain, which the same fire produced in him the same way, is *not* in the fire. Why are whiteness and coldness in snow, and pain not, when it produces the one and the other idea in us; and can do neither, but by the bulk, figure, number, and motion of its solid parts?

The particular bulk, number, figure, and motion of the parts of fire or snow are really in them, whether any one's senses perceive them or no: and therefore they may be called *real* qualities, because they really exist in those bodies. But light, heat, whiteness, or coldness, are no more really in them than sickness or pain is in manna. Take away the sensation of them; let not the eyes see light or colours, nor the ears hear sounds; let the palate not taste, nor the nose smell, and all colours, tastes, odours, and sounds, *as they are such particular ideas*, vanish and cease, and are reduced to their causes, that is, bulk, figure, and motion of parts.

A piece of manna of a sensible bulk is able to produce in us the idea of a round or square figure; and by being removed from one place to another, the idea of motion. This idea of motion represents it as it really is in manna moving: a circle or square are the same, whether in idea or existence, in the mind or in the manna. And this, both motion and figure, are really in the manna, whether we take notice of them or no: this everybody is ready to agree to. Besides, manna, by the bulk, figure, texture, and motion of its parts, has a power to produce the sensations of sickness, and sometimes of acute pains or gripings in us. That these ideas of sickness and pain are *not* in the manna, but effects of its operations on us, and are nowhere when we feel them not; this also every one readily agrees to. And yet men are hardly to be brought to think that sweetness and whiteness are not really in manna; which are but the effects of the operations of manna, by the motion, size, and figure of its particles, on the eyes and palate: as the pain and sickness caused by manna are confessedly nothing but the effects of its operations on the stomach and guts, by the size, motion, and figure of its insensible parts, (for by nothing else can a body operate, as has been proved): as if it could not operate on the eyes and palate, and thereby produce in the mind particular distinct ideas, which in itself it has not, as well as we allow it can operate on the guts and stomach, and thereby produce distinct ideas, which in itself it has not. These ideas, being all effects of the operations of manna on several parts of our bodies, by the size, figure, number, and motion of its parts; why those produced by the eyes and palate should rather be thought to be really in the manna, than those produced by the stomach and guts; or why the pain and sickness, ideas that are the effect of manna, should be thought to be nowhere when they are not felt; and yet the sweetness and whiteness, effects of the same manna on other parts of the body, by ways equally as unknown, should be thought to exist in the manna, when they are not seen or tasted, would need some reason to explain.

Let us consider the red and white colours in porphyry. Hinder light from striking on it, and its colours vanish; it no longer produces any such ideas in us: upon the return of light it produces these appearances on us again. Can any one think any real alterations are made in the porphyry by the presence or absence of light; and that those ideas of whiteness and redness are really in porphyry in the light, when it is plain *it has no colour in the dark?* It has, indeed, such a configuration of particles, both night and day, as are apt, by the rays of light rebounding from some parts of that hard stone, to produce in us the idea of redness, and from others the idea of whiteness; but whiteness or redness are not in it at any time, but such a texture that hath the power to produce such a sensation in us.

Pound an almond, and the clear white colour will be altered into a dirty one, and the sweet taste into an oily one. What real alteration can the beating of the pestle make in any body, but an alteration of the texture of it?

Ideas being thus distinguished and understood, we may be able to give an account how the same water, at the same time, may produce the idea of cold by one hand and of heat by the other: whereas it is impossible that the same water, if those ideas were really in it, should at the same time be both hot and cold. For, if we imagine *warmth,* as it is in our hands, to be nothing but a certain sort and degree of motion in the minute particles of our nerves or animal spirits, we may understand how it is possible that the same water may, at the same time, produce the sensations of heat in one hand and cold in the other; which yet *figure* never does, that never producing the idea of a square by one hand which has produced the idea of a globe by another. But if the sensation of heat and cold be nothing but the increase or diminution of the motion of the minute parts of our bodies, caused by the corpuscles of any other body, it is easy to be understood, that if that motion be greater in one hand than in the other; if a body be applied to the two hands, which has in its minute particles a greater motion than in those of one of the hands, and a less than in those of the other, it will increase the motion of the one hand and lessen it in the other; and so cause the different sensations of heat and cold that depend thereon.

I have in what just goes before been engaged in physical inquiries a little further than perhaps I intended. But, it being necessary to make the nature of sensation a little understood; and to make the difference between the *qualities* in bodies, and the *ideas* produced by them in the mind, to be distinctly conceived, without which it were impossible to discourse intelligibly of them; I hope I shall be pardoned this little excursion into natural philosophy; it being necessary in our present inquiry to distinguish the *primary* and *real* qualities of bodies, which are always in them (namely, solidity, extension, figure, number, and motion, or rest, and are sometimes perceived by us, namely, when the bodies they are in are big enough singly to be discerned), from those *secondary* and *imputed* qualities, which are but the powers of several combinations of those primary ones, when they operate without being distinctly discerned; whereby we may also come to know what ideas are, and what are not, resemblances of something really existing in the bodies we denominate from them.

The qualities, then, that are in bodies, rightly considered, are of three sorts:—

First, The bulk, figure, number, situation, and motion or rest of their solid parts. Those are in them, whether we perceive them or not; and when they are of that size that we can discover them, we have by these an idea of the thing as it is in itself; as is plain in artificial things. These I call *primary qualities.*

Secondly, The power that is in any body, by reason of its insensible primary qualities, to operate after a peculiar manner on any of our senses, and thereby produce in *us* the different ideas of several colours, sounds, smells, tastes, and so forth. These are usually called *sensible qualities.*

Thirdly, The power that is in any body, by reason of the particular constitution of its primary qualities, to make such a change in the bulk, figure, texture, and motion of *another body,* as to make it operate on our senses differently from what it did before. Thus the sun has a power to make wax white, and fire to make lead fluid. These are usually called *powers.*

The first of these, as has been said, I think may be properly called real, original, or primary qualities; because they are in the things themselves, whether they are perceived or not: and upon their different modifications it is that the secondary qualities depend.

The other two are only powers to act differently upon other things: which powers result from the different modifications of those primary qualities.

But, though the two latter sorts of qualities are powers barely, and nothing but powers, relating to several other bodies, and resulting from the different modifications of the original qualities, yet they are generally otherwise thought of. For the *second* sort, namely, the powers to produce several ideas in us, by our senses, are looked upon as real qualities in the things thus affecting us: but the *third* sort are called and esteemed barely powers. For example. The idea of heat or light, which we receive by our eyes, or touch, from the sun, are commonly thought real qualities existing in the sun, and something more than mere powers in it. But when we consider the sun in reference to wax, which it melts or blanches, we look on the whiteness and softness produced in the wax, not as qualities in the sun, but effects produced by powers in it. Whereas, if rightly considered, these qualities of light and warmth, which are perceptions in me when I am warmed or enlightened by the sun, are no otherwise in the sun, than the changes made in the wax, when it is blanched or melted, are in the sun. They are all of them equally *powers in the sun, depending on its primary qualities*; whereby it is able, in the one case, so to alter the bulk, figure, texture, or motion of some of the insensible parts of my eyes or hands, as thereby to produce in me the idea of light or heat; and in the other, it is able so to alter the bulk, figure, texture, or motion of the insensible parts of the wax, as to make them fit to produce in me the distinct ideas of white and fluid.

The reason why the one are ordinarily taken for real qualities, and the other only for bare powers, seems to be, because the ideas we have of distinct colours, sounds, and so forth, containing nothing at all in them of bulk, figure, or motion, we are not apt to think them the effects of these primary qualities; which appear not, to our senses, to operate in their production, and with which they have not any apparent congruity or conceivable connexion. Hence it is that we are so forward to imagine, that those ideas are the resemblances of something really existing in the objects themselves: since sensation discovers nothing of bulk, figure, or motion of parts in their production; nor can reason show how bodies, *by their bulk, figure, and motion,* should produce in the mind the ideas of blue or yellow, and so forth. But, in the other case, in the operations of bodies changing the qualities one of another, we plainly discover that the quality produced hath commonly no resemblance with anything in the thing producing it; wherefore we look on it as a bare effect of power. For, through receiving the idea of heat or light from the sun, we are apt to think *it* is a perception and resemblance of such a quality in the sun; yet when we see wax, or a fair face, receive change of colour from the sun, we cannot imagine *that* to be the reception or resemblance of anything in the sun, because we find not those different colours in the sun itself. For, our senses being able to observe a likeness or unlikeness of sensible qualities in two different external objects, we forwardly enough conclude the production of any sensible quality in any subject to be an effect of bare power, and not the communication of any quality which was really in the efficient, when we find no such sensible quality in the thing that produced it. But our senses, not being able to discover any unlikeness between the idea produced in us, and the quality of the object producing it, we are apt to imagine that our ideas are resemblances of something in the objects, and not the effects of certain powers placed in the modification of their primary qualities, with which primary quality the ideas produced in us have no resemblance.

To conclude. Beside those before-mentioned primary qualities in bodies, namely, bulk, figure, extension, number, and motion of their solid parts; all the rest, whereby we take notice of bodies, and distinguish them one from another, are nothing else but several powers in them, depending on those primary qualities; whereby they are fitted, either by immediately operating on our bodies to produce several different ideas in us; or else, by operating on other bodies, so to change their primary qualities as to render them capable of producing ideas in us different from what before they did. The former of these, I think, may be called secondary qualities *immediately perceivable*: the latter, secondary qualities, *mediately perceivable*.

(3) KNOWLEDGE

Since the mind, in all its thoughts and reasonings, hath no other immediate object but its own ideas, which it alone does or can contemplate, it is evident that our knowledge is only conversant about them.

Knowledge then seems to me to be nothing but *the perception of the connexion of an agreement, or disagreement and repugnancy of any of our ideas*. In this alone it consists. Where this perception is, there is knowledge, and where it is not, there, though we may fancy, guess, or believe, yet we always come short of knowledge. For when we know that white is not black, what do we else but perceive, that these two ideas do not agree? When we possess ourselves with the utmost security of the demonstration, that the three angles of a triangle are equal to two right ones, what do we more but perceive, that equality to two right ones does necessarily agree to, and is inseparable from, the three angles of a triangle?

.   .   .   .

All our knowledge consisting, as I have said, in the view the mind has of its own ideas, which is the utmost light and greatest certainty we, with our faculties, and in our way of knowledge, are capable of, it may not be amiss to consider a little the degrees of its evidence. The different clearness of our knowledge seems to me to lie in the different way of perception the mind has of the agreement or disagreement of any of its ideas. For if we will reflect on our own ways of thinking, we will find, that sometimes the mind perceives the agreement or disagreement of two ideas *immediately by themselves,* without the intervention of any other: and this I think we may call *intuitive knowledge.* For in this the mind is at no pains of proving or examining, but perceives the truth as the eye doth light, only by being directed towards it. Thus the mind perceives that *white* is not *black,* that a *circle* is not a *triangle,* that *three* are more than *two* and equal to *one and two.* Such kinds of truths the mind perceives at the first sight of the ideas together, by bare intuition; without the intervention of any other idea: and this kind of knowledge is the clearest and most certain that human frailty is capable of. This part of knowledge is irresistible, and, like bright sunshine, forces itself immediately to be perceived, as soon as ever the mind turns its view that way; and leaves no room for hesitation, doubt, or examination, but the mind is presently filled with the clear light of it. *It is on this intuition that depends all the certainty and evidence of all our knowledge*; which certainty every one finds to be so great, that he cannot imagine, and therefore not require a greater: for a man cannot conceive himself capable of a greater certainty than to know that any idea in his mind is such as he perceives it to be; and that two ideas, wherein he perceives a difference, are different and not precisely the same. He that demands a greater certainty than this, demands he knows not what, and shows only that he has a mind to be a sceptic, without being able to be so. Certainty depends so wholly on this intuition, that, in the next degree of knowledge which I call demonstrative, this intuition is necessary in all the connexions of the intermediate ideas, without which we cannot attain knowledge and certainty.

The next degree of knowledge is, where the mind perceives the agreement or disagreement and any ideas, but not immediately. Though wherever the mind perceives the agreement or disagreement of any of its ideas, there be certain knowledge; yet it does not always happen, that the mind sees that agreement or disagreement, which there is between them, even where it is discoverable; and in that case remains in ignorance, and at most gets no further than a probable conjecture. The reason why the mind cannot always perceive presently the agreement or disagreement of two ideas, is, because those ideas, concerning whose agreement or disagreement the inquiry is made, cannot by the mind be so put together as to show it. In this case then, when the mind cannot so bring its ideas together as by their immediate comparison, and as it were juxtaposition or application one to another, to perceive their agreement or disagreement, it is fain, *by the intervention of other ideas* (one or more, as it happens) to discover the agreement or disagreement which it searches; and this is that which we call *reasoning*. Thus, the mind being willing to know the agreement or disagreement in bigness between the three angles of a triangle and two right ones, cannot by an immediate view and comparing them do it: because the three angles of a triangle cannot be brought at once, and be compared with any other one, or two, angles; and so of this the mind has no immediate, no intuitive knowledge. In this case the mind is fain to find out some other angles, to which the three angles of a triangle have an equality; and, finding those equal to two right ones, comes to know their equality to two right ones.

Those intervening ideas, which serve to show the agreement of any two others, are called *proofs;* and where the agreement and disagreement is by this means plainly and clearly perceived, it is called *demonstration;* it being *shown* to the understanding, and the mind made to see that it is so. A quickness in the mind to find out these intermediate ideas, (that shall discover the agreement or disagreement of any other,) and to apply them right, is, I suppose, that which is called *sagacity*.

This knowledge, by intervening proofs, though it be certain, yet the evidence of it is not altogether so clear and bright, nor the assent so ready, as in intuitive knowledge. For, though in demonstration the mind does at last perceive the agreement or disagreement of the ideas it considers; yet it is not without pains and attention: there must be more than one transient view to find it. A steady application and pursuit are required to this discovery: and there must be a progression by steps and degrees, before the mind can in this way arrive at certainty, and come to perceive the agreement or repugnancy between two ideas that need proofs and the use of reason to show it.

Another difference between intuitive and demonstrative knowledge is, that, though in the latter all doubt be removed when, by the intervention of the intermediate ideas, the agreement or disagreement is perceived, yet before the demonstration there was a doubt; which in intuitive knowledge cannot happen to the mind that has its faculty of perception left to a degree capable of distinct ideas; no more than it can be a doubt to the eye (that can distinctly see white and black), whether this ink and this paper be all of a colour. If there be sight in the eyes, it will, at first glimpse, without hesitation, perceive the words printed on this paper different from the colour of the paper: and so if the mind have the faculty of distinct perception, it will perceive the agreement or disagreement of those ideas that produce intuitive knowledge. If the eyes have lost the faculty of seeing, or the mind of perceiving, we in vain inquire after the quickness of sight in one, or clearness of perception in the other.

It is true, the perception produced by demonstration is also very clear; yet it is often with a great abatement of that evident lustre and full assurance that always accompany that which I call intuitive: like a face reflected by several mirrors one to another, where, as long as it retains the similitude and agreement with the object, it produces a knowledge; but it is still, in every successive reflection, with a lessening of that perfect clearness and distinctness which is in the first; till at last, after many removes, it has a great mixture of dimness, and is not at first sight so knowable, especially to weak eyes. Thus it is with knowledge made out by a long train of proof.

Now, in every step reason makes in demonstrative knowledge, there is an intuitive knowledge of that agreement or disagreement it seeks with the next intermediate idea which it uses as a proof: for if it were not so, that yet would need a proof; since without the perception of such agreement or disagreement, there is no knowledge produced: if it be perceived by itself, it is intuitive knowledge: if it cannot be perceived by itself, there is need of some intervening idea, as a common measure, to show their agreement or disagreement. By which it is plain, that every step in reasoning that produces knowledge, has intuitive certainty; which when the mind perceives, there is no more required but to remember it, to make the agreement or disagreement of the ideas concerning which we inquire visible and certain. So that to make anything a demonstration, it is necessary to perceive the immediate agreement of the intervening ideas, whereby the agreement or disagreement of the two ideas under examination (whereof the one is always the first, and the other the last in the account) is found. This intuitive perception of the agreement or disagreement of the intermediate ideas, in each step and progression of the demonstration, must also be carried exactly in the mind, and a man must be sure that no part is left out: which, because in long deductions, and the use of many proofs, the memory does not always so readily and exactly retain; therefore it comes to pass, that this is more imperfect than intuitive knowledge, and men embrace often falsehood for demonstrations.

·　　·　　·　　·　　·　　·　　·　　·　　·　　·　　·　　·

These two, namely, intuition and demonstration, are the degrees of our *knowledge;* whatever comes short of one of these, with what assurance soever embraced, is but *faith* or *opinion,* but not knowledge, at least in all general truths. There is, indeed, another perception of the mind, employed about *the particular existence of finite beings without us,* which, going beyond bare probability, and yet not reaching perfectly to either of the foregoing degrees of certainty, passes under the name of *knowledge.* There can be nothing more certain than that the idea we receive from an external object is in our minds: this is intuitive knowledge. But whether there be anything more than barely that idea in our minds; whether we can thence certainly infer the existence of anything without us, which corresponds to that idea, is that whereof some men think there may be a question made; because men may have such ideas in their minds, when no such thing exists, no such object affects their senses. But yet here I think we are provided with an evidence that puts us past doubting. For I ask any one, Whether he be not invincibly conscious to himself of a different perception, when he looks on the sun by day, and thinks on it by night; when he actually tastes wormwood, or smells a rose, or only thinks on that savour or odour? We as plainly find the difference there is between any idea revived in our minds by our own memory, and actually coming into our minds by our senses, as we do between any two distinct ideas. If any one say, a dream may do the same thing, and all these ideas may be produced in us without any external objects; he may please to dream that I make him this answer: (1) That it is no great matter, whether I remove his scruple or no: where all is but dream, reasoning and arguments are of no use, truth and knowledge nothing. (2) That I believe he will allow a very manifest difference between dreaming of being in the fire, and being actually in it. But yet if he be resolved to appear so sceptical as to maintain, that what I call being actually in the fire is nothing but a dream; and that we cannot thereby certainly know, that any such thing as fire actually exists without us: I answer, That we certainly finding that pleasure or pain follows upon the application of certain objects to us, whose existence we perceive, or dream that we perceive, by our senses; this certainty is as great as our happiness or misery, beyond which we have no concernment to know or to be. So that, I think, we may add to the two former sorts of knowledge this also, of the existence of particular external objects, by that perception and consciousness we have of the actual entrance of ideas from them, and allow these three degrees of knowledge, namely, *intuitive, demonstrative,* and *sensitive*: in each of which there are different degrees and ways of evidence and certainty.

• • • • • • • • • • • •

The knowledge of our own being we have by intuition. The existence of a God, reason clearly makes known to us, as has been shown.

The knowledge of the existence of *any other thing* we can have only by *sensation:* for there being no necessary connexion of real existence with any *idea* a man hath in his memory; nor of any other existence but that of God with the existence of any particular man: no particular man can know the existence of any other being, but only when, by actual operating upon him, it makes itself perceived by him. For, the having the idea of anything in our mind, no more proves the existence of that thing, than the picture of a man evidences his being in the world, or the visions of a dream make thereby a true history.

It is therefore the *actual receiving* of ideas from without that gives us notice of the existence of other things, and makes us know, that something doth exist at that time without us, which causes that idea in us; though perhaps we neither know nor consider how it does it. For it takes not from the certainty of our senses, and the ideas we receive by them, that we know not the manner wherein they are produced: for example, whilst I write this, I have, by the paper affecting my eyes, that idea produced in my mind, which, whatever object causes, I call *white;* by which I know that that quality or accident (*i.e.,* whose appearance before my eyes always causes that idea) doth really exist, and hath a being without me. And of this, the greatest assurance I can possibly have, and to which my faculties can attain, is the testimony of my eyes, which are the proper and sole judges of this thing; whose testimony I have reason to rely on as so certain, that I can no more doubt, whilst I write this, that I see white and black, and that something really exists that causes that sensation in me, than that I write or move my hand; which is a certainty as great as human nature is capable of, concerning the existence of anything, but a man's self alone, and of God.

The notice we have by our senses of the existing of things without us, though it be not altogether so certain as our intuitive knowledge, or the deductions of our reason employed about the clear abstract ideas of our own minds; yet it is an assurance that deserves the name of *knowledge*. If we persuade ourselves that our faculties act and inform us right concerning the existence of those objects that affect them, it cannot pass for an ill-grounded confidence: for I think nobody can, in earnest, be so sceptical as to be uncertain of the existence of those things which he sees and feels. At least, he that can doubt so far, (whatever he may have with his own thoughts) will never have any controversy with me; since he can never be sure I say anything contrary to his own opinion. As to myself, I think God has given me assurance enough of the existence of things without me: since, by their different application, I can produce in myself both pleasure and pain, which is one great concernment of my present state. This is certain: the confidence that our faculties do not herein deceive us, is the greatest assurance we are capable of concerning the existence of material beings. For we cannot act anything but by our faculties; nor talk of knowledge itself, but by the help of those faculties which are fitted to apprehend even what knowledge is.

But besides the assurance we have from our senses themselves, that they do not err in the information they give us of the existence of things without us, when they are affected by them, we are further confirmed in this assurance by other concurrent reasons:

(I) It is plain those perceptions are produced in us by exterior causes affecting our senses: because those that want the *organs* of any sense, never can have the ideas belonging to that sense produced in their minds. This is too evident to be doubted: and therefore we cannot but be assured that they come in by the organs of that sense, and no other way. The organs themselves, it is plain, do not produce them: for then the eyes of a man in the dark would produce colours, and his nose smell roses in the winter: but we see nobody gets the relish of a pineapple, till he goes to the Indies, where it is, and tastes it.

(II) Because sometimes I find that *I cannot avoid the having those ideas produced in my mind.* For though, when my eyes are shut, or windows fast, I can at pleasure recall to my mind the ideas of light, or the sun, which former sensations had lodged in my memory; so I can at pleasure lay by *that* idea, and take into my view that of the smell of a rose, or taste of sugar. But, if I turn my eyes at noon towards the sun, I cannot avoid the ideas which the light or sun then produces in me. So that there is a manifest difference between the ideas laid up in my memory, (over which, if they were there only, I should have constantly the same power to dispose of them, and lay them by at pleasure) and those which force themselves upon me, and I cannot avoid having. And therefore it must needs be some exterior cause, and the brisk acting of some objects without me, whose efficacy I cannot resist, that produces those ideas in my mind, whether I will or no. Besides, there is nobody who doth not perceive the difference in himself between contemplating the sun, as he hath the idea of it in his memory, and actually looking upon it: of which two, his perception is so distinct, that few of his ideas are more distinguishable one from another. And therefore he hath certain knowledge that they are not *both* memory, or the actions of his mind, and fancies only within him; but that actual seeing hath a cause without.

(III) Add to this, that many of those ideas are *produced in us with pain,* which afterwards we remember without the least offence. Thus, the pain of heat or cold, when the idea of it is revived in our minds, gives us no disturbance; which, when felt, was very troublesome; and is again, when actually repeated: which is occasioned by the disorder the external object causes in our bodies when applied to them: and we remember the pains of hunger, thirst, or the headache, without any pain at all; which would either never disturb us, or else constantly do it, as often as we thought of it, were there nothing more but ideas floating in our minds, and appearances entertaining our fancies, without the real existence of things affecting us from abroad. The same may be said of *pleasure,* accompanying several actual sensations. And though mathematical demonstration depends not upon sense, yet the examining them by diagrams gives great credit to the evidence of our sight, and seems to give it a certainty approaching to that of demonstration itself. For, it would be very strange, that a man should allow it for an undeniable truth, that two angles of a figure, which he measures by lines and angles of a diagram, should be bigger one than the other, and yet doubt of the existence of those lines and angles, which by looking on he makes use of to measure that by.

(IV) Our *senses* in many cases *bear witness to the truth of each other's report,* concerning the existence of sensible things without us. He that *sees* a fire, may, if he doubt whether it be anything more than a bare fancy, *feel* it too; and be convinced, by putting his hand in it. Which certainly could never be put into such exquisite pain by a bare idea or phantom, unless that the pain be a fancy too: which yet he cannot, when the burn is well, by raising the idea of it, bring upon himself again.

Thus I see, whilst I write this, I can change the appearance of the paper; and by designing the letters, tell *beforehand* what new idea it shall exhibit the very next moment, by barely drawing my pen over it: which will neither appear (let me fancy as much as I will) if my hands stand still; or though I move my pen, if my eyes be shut: nor, when those characters are once made on the paper, can I choose afterwards but see them as they are; that is, have the ideas of such letters as I have made. Whence it is manifest, that they are not barely the sport and play of my own imagination, when I find that the characters that were made at the pleasure of my own thoughts, do not obey them; nor yet cease to be, whenever I shall fancy it, but continue to affect my senses constantly and regularly, according to the figures I made them. To which if we will add, that the sight of those shall, from another man, draw such sounds as I beforehand design they shall stand for, there will be little reason left to doubt that those words I write do really exist without me, when they cause a long series of regular sounds to affect my ears, which could not be the effect of my imagination, nor could my memory retain them in that order.

But yet, if after all this any one will be so sceptical as to distrust his senses, and to affirm that all we see and hear, feel and taste, think and do, during our whole being, is but the series and deluding appearances of a long dream, whereof there is no reality; and therefore will question the existence of all things, or our knowledge of anything: I must desire him to consider, that, if all be a dream, then he doth but dream that he makes the question, and so it is not much matter that a waking man should answer him. But yet, if he pleases, he may dream that I make him this answer, That the certainty of things existing in *rerum natura* when we have the testimony of our senses for it is not only as great as our frame can attain to, but as our condition needs. For, our faculties being suited not to the full extent of being, nor to a perfect, clear, comprehensive knowledge of things free from all doubt and scruple; but to the preservation of us, in whom they are; and accommodated to the use of life: they serve to our purpose well enough, if they will but give us certain notice of those things, which are convenient or inconvenient to us. For he that sees a candle burning, and hath experimented the force of its flame by putting his finger in it, will little doubt that this is something existing without him, which does him harm, and puts him to great pain: which is assurance enough, when no man requires greater certainty to govern his actions by than what is as certain as his actions themselves. And if our dreamer pleases to try whether the glowing heat of a glass furnace be barely a wandering imagination in a drowsy man's fancy, by putting his hand into it, he may perhaps be wakened into a certainty greater than he could wish, that it is something more than bare imagination. So that this evidence is as great as we can desire, being as certain to us as our pleasure or pain, that is, happiness or misery; beyond which we have no concernment, either of knowing or being. Such an assurance of the existence of things without us is sufficient to direct us in the attaining the good and avoiding the evil which is caused by them, which is the important concernment we have of being made acquainted with them.

In fine, then, when our senses do actually convey into our understandings any idea, we cannot but be satisfied that there doth something *at that time* really exist without us, which doth affect our senses, and by them give notice of itself to our apprehensive faculties, and actually produce that idea which we then perceive: and we cannot so far distrust their testimony, as to doubt that such *collections* of simple ideas as we have observed by our senses to be united together, do really exist together. But this knowledge extends as far as the present testimony of our senses, employed about particular objects that do then affect them, and no further. For if I saw such a collection of simple ideas as is wont to be called *man,* existing together one minute since, and am now alone, I cannot be certain that the same man exists now, since there is no *necessary connexion* of his existence a minute since with his existence now: by a thousand ways he may cease to be, since I had the testimony of my senses for his existence. And if I cannot be certain that the man I saw last today is now in being, I can less be certain that he is so who hath been longer removed from my senses, and I have not seen since yesterday, or since the last year: and much less can I be certain of the existence of men that I never saw. And, therefore, though it be highly probable that millions of men do now exist, yet, whilst I am alone, writing this, I have not that certainty of it which we strictly call knowledge; though the great likelihood of it puts me past doubt, and it be reasonable for me to do several things upon the confidence that there are men (and men also of my acquaintance, with whom I have to do) now in the world: but this is but probability, not knowledge.

Whereby yet we may observe how foolish and vain a thing it is for a man of a narrow knowledge, who having reason given him to judge of the different evidence and probability of things, and to be swayed accordingly; how vain, I say, it is to expect demonstration and certainty in things not capable of it; and refuse assent to very rational propositions, and act contrary to very plain and clear truths, because they cannot be made out so evident, as to surmount every the least (I will not say reason, but) pretence of doubting. He that, in the ordinary affairs of life, would admit of nothing but direct plain demonstration, would be sure of nothing in this world, but of perishing quickly. The wholesomeness of his meat or drink would not give him reason to venture on it: and I would fain know what it is he could do upon such grounds as are capable of no doubt, no objection.

Critique and Revision
of Locke's Empiricism

~~~~~~

(1) It is evident to anyone who takes a survey of the objects of human knowledge, that they are either ideas actually imprinted on the senses, or else such as are perceived by attending to the passions and operations of the mind, or lastly ideas formed by help of memory and imagination, either compounding, dividing, or barely representing those originally perceived in the aforesaid ways. By sight I have the ideas of light and colours with their several degrees and variations. By touch I perceive, for example, hard and soft, heat and cold, motion and resistance, and of all these more and less either as to quantity or degree. Smelling furnishes me with odours, the palate with tastes, and hearing conveys sounds to the mind in all their variety of tone and composition. And as several of these are observed to accompany each other, they come to be marked by one name, and so to be reputed as one thing. Thus, for example, a certain colour, taste, smell, figure and consistence having been observed to go together, are accounted one distinct thing, signified by the name *apple*. Other collections of ideas constitute a stone, a tree, a book, and the like sensible things; which, as they are pleasing or disagreeable, excite the passions of love, hatred, joy, grief, and so forth.

(2) But besides all that endless variety of ideas or objects of knowledge, there is likewise something which knows or perceives them, and exercises divers operations, as willing, imagining, remember-

* This selection is from Berkeley's *A Treatise Concerning the Principles of Human Knowledge.*

ing about them. This perceiving, active being is what I call *mind, spirit, soul* or *my self*. By which words I do not denote any one of my ideas, but a thing entirely distinct from them, wherein they exist, or, which is the same thing, whereby they are perceived; for the existence of an idea consists in being perceived.

(3) That neither our thoughts, nor passions, nor ideas formed by the imagination, exist without the mind, is what everybody will allow. And it seems no less evident that the various sensations or ideas imprinted on the sense, however blended or combined together (that is, whatever objects they compose) cannot exist otherwise than in a mind perceiving them. I think an intuitive knowledge may be obtained of this by anyone that shall attend to what is meant by the term *exist* when applied to sensible things. The table I write on, I say, exists, that is, I see and feel it; and if I were out of my study I should say it existed, meaning thereby that if I was in my study I might perceive it, or that some other spirit actually does perceive it. There was an odour, that is, it was smelled; there was a sound, that is to say, it was heard; a colour or figure, and it was perceived by sight or touch. This is all that I can understand by these and the like expressions. For as to what is said of the absolute existence of unthinking things without any relation to their being perceived, that seems perfectly unintelligible. Their *esse* is *percipi,* nor is it possible they should have any existence out of the minds or thinking things which perceive them.

(4) It is indeed an opinion strangely prevailing amongst men, that houses, mountains, rivers, and in a word all sensible objects, have an existence natural or real, distinct from their being perceived by the understanding. But with how great an assurance and acquiescence soever this principle may be entertained in the world; yet whoever shall find in his heart to call it in question may, if I mistake not, perceive it to involve a manifest contradiction. For what are the forementioned objects but the things we perceive by sense, and what do we perceive besides our own ideas or sensations; and is it not plainly repugnant that any one of these or any combination of them should exist unperceived?

.   .   .   .

(6) Some truths there are so near and obvious to the mind that a man need only open his eyes to see them. Such I take this important

one to be, to wit, that all the choir of heaven and furniture of the earth, in a word all those bodies which compose the mighty frame of the world, have not any subsistence without a mind, that their being is to be perceived or known; that consequently so long as they are not actually perceived by me, or do not exist in my mind or that of any other created spirit, they must either have no existence at all, or else subsist in the mind of some eternal spirit: it being perfectly unintelligible and involving all the absurdity of abstraction, to attribute to any single part of them an existence independent of a spirit. To be convinced of which, the reader need only reflect and try to separate in his own thoughts the being of a sensible thing from its being perceived.

(7) From what has been said, it follows, there is not any other substance than *spirit,* or that which perceives. But for the fuller proof of this point, let it be considered, the sensible qualities are colour, figure, motion, smell, taste, and such like, that is, the ideas perceived by sense. Now for an idea to exist in an unperceiving thing is a manifest contradiction; for to have an idea is all one as to perceive: that therefore wherein colour, figure, and the like qualities exist, must perceive them; hence it is clear there can be no unthinking substance or *substratum* of those ideas.

(8) But, say you, though the ideas themselves do not exist without the mind, yet there may be things like them whereof they are copies or resemblances, which things exist without the mind, in an unthinking substance. I answer, an idea can be like nothing but an idea; a colour or figure can be like nothing but another colour or figure. If we look but ever so little into our thoughts, we shall find it impossible for us to conceive a likeness except only between our ideas. Again, I ask whether those supposed originals or external things, of which our ideas are the pictures or representations, be themselves perceivable or no? If they are, then they are ideas, and we have gained our point; but if you say they are not, I appeal to anyone whether it be sense to assert a colour is like something which is invisible; hard or soft, like something which is intangible; and so of the rest.

(9) Some there are who make a distinction betwixt *primary* and *secondary* qualities: by the former, they mean extension, figure, motion, rest, solidity, or impenetrability, and number: by the latter they denote all other sensible qualities, as colours, sounds, tastes,

and so forth. The ideas we have of these they acknowledge not to be the resemblances of any thing existing without the mind or unperceived; but they will have our ideas of the primary qualities to be patterns or images of things which exist without the mind, in an unthinking substance which they call *matter*. By matter therefore we are to understand an inert, senseless substance, in which extension, figure, and motion do actually subsist. But it is evident from what we have already shown, that extension, figure and motion are only ideas existing in the mind, and that an idea can be like nothing but another idea, and that consequently neither they nor their archetypes can exist in an unperceiving substance. Hence it is plain that the very notion of what is called *matter* or *corporeal substance* involves a contradiction in it.

(10) They who assert that figure, motion, and the rest of the primary or original qualities do exist without the mind, in unthinking substances, do at the same time acknowledge that colours, sounds, heat, cold, and suchlike secondary qualities, do not, which they tell us are sensations existing in the mind alone, that depend on and are occasioned by the different size, texture and motion of the minute particles of matter. This they take for an undoubted truth, which they can demonstrate beyond all exception. Now if it be certain, that those original qualities are inseparably united with the other sensible qualities, and not even in thought capable of being abstracted from them, it plainly follows that they exist only in the mind. But I desire any one to reflect and try, whether he can by any abstraction of thought conceive the extension and motion of a body without all other sensible qualities. For my own part, I see evidently that it is not in my power to frame an idea of a body extended and moved, but I must withal give it some colour or other sensible quality which is acknowledged to exist only in the mind. In short, extension, figure, and motion, abstracted from all other qualities, are inconceivable. Where therefore the other sensible qualities are, there must these be also, to wit, in the mind and nowhere else.

.   .   .   .

(14) I shall farther add, that after the same manner as modern philosophers prove certain sensible qualities to have no existence

in matter, or without the mind, the same thing may be likewise proved of all other sensible qualities whatsoever. Thus, for instance, it is said that heat and cold are affections only of the mind, and not at all patterns of real beings existing in the corporeal substances which excite them, for that the same body which appears cold to one hand seems warm to another. Now why may we not as well argue that figure and extension are not patterns or resemblances of qualities existing in matter, because to the same eye at different stations, or eyes of a different texture at the same station, they appear various, and cannot therefore be the images of anything settled and determinate without the mind? Again, it is proved that sweetness is not really in the sapid thing, because the thing remaining unaltered the sweetness is changed into bitter, as in case of a fever or otherwise vitiated palate. Is it not as reasonable to say, that motion is not without the mind, since if the succession of ideas in the mind become swifter, the motion, it is acknowledged, shall appear slower without any alteration in any external object.

(15) In short, let anyone consider those arguments, which are thought manifestly to prove that colours and tastes exist only in the mind, and he shall find they may with equal force be brought to prove the same thing of extension, figure, and motion. Though it must be confessed this method of arguing doth not so much prove that there is no extension or colour in an outward object, as that we do not know by sense which is the true extension or colour of the object. But the arguments foregoing plainly show it to be impossible that any colour or extension at all, or other sensible quality whatsoever, should exist in an unthinking subject without the mind, or in truth that there should be any such thing as an outward object.

(16) But let us examine a little the received opinion. It is said extension is a mode or accident of matter, and that matter is the *substratum* that supports it. Now I desire that you would explain what is meant by matter's *supporting* extension: say you, I have no idea of matter, and therefore cannot explain it. I answer, though you have no positive, yet if you have any meaning at all, you must at least have a relative idea of matter; though you know not what it is, yet you must be supposed to know what relation it bears to accidents, and what is meant by its supporting them. It is evident

support cannot here be taken in its usual or literal sense, as when we say that pillars support a building: in what sense therefore must it be taken?

(17) If we inquire into what the most accurate philosophers declare themselves to mean by *material substance,* we shall find them acknowledge, they have no other meaning annexed to those sounds, but the idea of being in general, together with the relative notion of its supporting accidents. The general idea of being appeareth to me the most abstract and incomprehensible of all other; and as for its supporting accidents, this, as we have just now observed, cannot be understood in the common sense of those words; it must therefore be taken in some other sense, but what that is they do not explain. So that when I consider the two parts or branches which make the signification of the words *material substance* I am convinced there is no distinct meaning annexed to them. But why should we trouble ourselves any farther, in discussing this material *substratum* or support of figure and motion, and other sensible qualities? Does it not suppose they have an existence without the mind? And is not this a direct repugnancy, and altogether inconceivable?

(18) But though it were possible that solid, figured, movable substances may exist without the mind, corresponding to the ideas we have of bodies, yet how is it possible for us to know this? Either we must know it by sense, or by reason. As for our senses, by them we have the knowledge only of our sensations, ideas, or those things that are immediately perceived by sense, call them what you will: but they do not inform us that things exist without the mind, or unperceived, like to those which are perceived. This the materialists themselves acknowledge. It remains therefore that if we have any knowledge at all of external things, it must be by reason, inferring their existence from what is immediately perceived by sense. But what reason can induce us to believe the existence of bodies without the mind, from what we perceive, since the very patrons of matter themselves do not pretend there is any necessary connexion betwixt them and our ideas? I say it is granted on all hands (and what happens in dreams, frenzies, and the like, puts it beyond dispute) that it is possible we might be affected with all the ideas we have now, though no bodies existed without, resembling them. Hence it is evident the supposition of external bodies is not necessary for the

producing our ideas, since it is granted they are produced sometimes, and might possibly be produced always in the same order we see them in at present, without their concurrence.

(19) But though we might possibly have all our sensations without them, yet perhaps it may be thought easier to conceive and explain the manner of their production, by supposing external bodies in their likeness rather than otherwise; and so it might be at least probable there are such things as bodies that excite their ideas in our minds. But neither can this be said; for though we give the materialists their external bodies, they by their own confession are never the nearer knowing how our ideas are produced: since they own themselves unable to comprehend in what manner body can act upon spirit, or how it is possible it should imprint any idea in the mind. Hence it is evident the production of ideas or sensations in our minds can be no reason why we should suppose matter or corporeal substances, since that is acknowledged to remain equally inexplicable with or without this supposition. If therefore it were possible for bodies to exist without the mind, yet to hold they do so, must needs be a very precarious opinion; since it is to suppose, without any reason at all, that God has created innumerable beings that are entirely useless, and serve to no manner of purpose.

. . . .

(22) I am afraid I have given cause to think me needlessly prolix in handling this subject. For to what purpose is it to dilate on that which may be demonstrated with the utmost evidence in a line or two, to anyone that is capable of the least reflexion? It is but looking into your own thoughts, and so trying whether you can conceive it possible for a sound, or figure, or motion, or colour, to exist without the mind, or unperceived. This easy trial may make you see, that what you contend for is a downright contradiction. Insomuch that I am content to put the whole upon this issue; if you can but conceive it possible for one extended movable substance, or in general, for any one idea or anything like an idea, to exist otherwise than in a mind perceiving it, I shall readily give up the cause: and as for all that *compages* of external bodies which you contend for, I shall grant you its existence, though you cannot either give me any reason why you believe it exists, or assign any use to it when it

is supposed to exist. I say, the bare possibility of your opinion's being true, shall pass for an argument that it is so.

(23) But say you, surely there is nothing easier than to imagine trees, for instance, in a park, or books existing in a closet, and nobody by to perceive them. I answer, you may so, there is no difficulty in it: but what is all this, I beseech you, more than framing in your mind certain ideas which you call *books* and *trees,* and at the same time omitting to frame the idea of anyone that may perceive them? But do not you yourself perceive or think of them all the while? This therefore is nothing to the purpose: it only shows you have the power of imagining or forming ideas in your mind; but it doth not show that you can conceive it possible the objects of your thought may exist without the mind: to make out this, it is necessary that you conceive them existing unconceived or unthought of, which is a manifest repugnancy. When we do our utmost to conceive the existence of external bodies, we are all the while only contemplating our own ideas. But the mind taking no notice of itself is deluded to think it can and doth conceive bodies existing unthought of or without the mind; though at the same time they are apprehended by or exist in itself. A little attention will discover to anyone the truth and evidence of what is here said, and make it unnecessary to insist on any other proofs against the existence of material substance.

(24) It is very obvious, upon the least inquiry into our own thoughts, to know whether it be possible for us to understand what is meant by the *absolute existence of sensible objects in themselves, or without the mind.* To me it is evident those words mark out either a direct contradiction, or else nothing at all. And to convince others of this, I know no readier or fairer way than to entreat they would calmly attend to their own thoughts: and if by this attention, the emptiness or repugnancy of those expressions does appear, surely nothing more is requisite for their conviction. It is on this therefore that I insist, to wit, that the absolute existence of unthinking things are words without a meaning, or which include a contradiction. This is what I repeat and inculcate, and earnestly recommend to the attentive thoughts of the reader.

(25) All our ideas, sensations, or the things which we perceive, by whatsoever names they may be distinguished, are visibly inactive; there is nothing of power or agency included in them. So that one

idea or object of thought cannot produce, or make any alteration in, another. To be satisfied of the truth of this, there is nothing else requisite but a bare observation of our ideas. For since they and every part of them exist only in the mind, it follows that there is nothing in them but what is perceived. But whoever shall attend to his ideas, whether of sense or reflexion, will not perceive in them any power or activity; there is therefore no such thing contained in them. A little attention will discover to us that the very being of an idea implies passiveness and inertness in it, insomuch that it is impossible for an idea to do anything, or, strictly speaking, to be the cause of anything: neither can it be the resemblance or pattern of any active being, as is evident from Section 8. Whence it plainly follows that extension, figure and motion cannot be the cause of our sensations. To say, therefore, that these are the effects of powers resulting from the configuration, number, motion, and size of corpuscles, must certainly be false.

(26) We perceive a continual succession of ideas, some are anew excited, others are changed or totally disappear. There is therefore some cause of these ideas whereon they depend, and which produces and changes them. That this cause cannot be any quality or idea or combination of ideas, is clear from the preceding section. It must therefore be a substance; but it has been shown that there is no corporeal or material substance: it remains therefore that the cause of ideas is an incorporeal active substance or spirit.

(27) A spirit is one simple, undivided, active being: as it perceives ideas, it is called the *understanding,* and as it produces or otherwise operates about them, it is called the *will.* Hence there can be no idea formed of a soul or spirit: for all ideas whatever, being passive and inert (see Section 25), they cannot represent unto us, by way of image or likeness, that which acts. A little attention will make it plain to anyone, that to have an idea which shall be like that active principle of motion and change of ideas, is absolutely impossible. Such is the nature of *spirit* or that which acts, that it cannot be of itself perceived, but only by the effects which it produceth. If any man shall doubt of the truth of what is here delivered, let him but reflect and try if he can frame the idea of any power or active being: and whether he hath ideas of two principal powers, marked by the names *will* and *understanding,* distinct from each other as well as from a third idea of substance or being in

general, with a relative notion of its supporting or being the subject of the aforesaid powers, which is signified by the name *soul* or *spirit*. This is what some hold; but so far as I can see, the words *will, soul, spirit,* do not stand for different ideas, or in truth for any idea at all, but for something which is very different from ideas, and which being an agent cannot be like unto, or represented by, any idea whatsoever. Though it must be owned at the same time, that we have some notion of soul, spirit, and the operations of the mind, such as willing, loving, hating, inasmuch as we know or understand the meaning of those words.

(28) I find I can excite ideas in my mind at pleasure, and vary and shift the scene as oft as I think fit. It is no more than willing, and straightway this or that idea arises in my fancy: and by the same power it is obliterated, and makes way for another. This making and unmaking of ideas doth very properly denominate the mind active. Thus much is certain, and grounded on experience: but when we talk of unthinking agents, or of exciting ideas exclusive of volition, we only amuse ourselves with words.

(29) But whatever power I may have over my own thoughts, I find the ideas actually perceived by sense have not a like dependence on my will. When in broad daylight I open my eyes, it is not in my power to choose whether I shall see or no, or to determine what particular objects shall present themselves to my view; and so likewise as to the hearing and other senses, the ideas imprinted on them are not creatures of my will. There is therefore some other will or spirit that produces them.

(30) The ideas of sense are more strong, lively, and distinct than those of the imagination; they have likewise a steadiness, order, and coherence, and are not excited at random, as those which are the effects of human wills often are, but in a regular train or series, the admirable connexion whereof sufficiently testifies the wisdom and benevolence of its Author. Now the set rules or established methods, wherein the mind we depend on excites in us the ideas of sense, are called the *Laws of Nature*: and these we learn by experience, which teaches us that such and such ideas are attended with such and such other ideas, in the ordinary course of things.

(31) This gives us a sort of foresight, which enables us to regulate our actions for the benefit of life. And without this we should be eternally at a loss: we could not know how to act anything that

might procure us the least pleasure, or remove the least pain, of sense. That food nourishes, sleep refreshes, and fire warms us, that to sow in the seed time is the way to reap in the harvest, and, in general, that to obtain such or such ends, such or such means are conducive, all this we know, not by discovering any necessary connexion between our ideas, but only by the observation of the settled Laws of Nature, without which we should be all in uncertainty and confusion, and a grown man no more know how to manage himself in the affairs of life, than an infant just born.

(32) And yet this consistent uniform working, which so evidently displays the goodness and wisdom of that governing spirit whose will constitutes the Laws of Nature, is so far from leading our thoughts to him, that it rather sends them awandering after second causes. For when we perceive certain ideas of sense constantly followed by other ideas, and we know this is not of our doing, we forthwith attribute power and agency to the ideas themselves, and make one the cause of another, than which nothing can be more absurd and unintelligible. Thus, for example, having observed that when we perceive by sight a certain round luminous figure, we at the same time perceive by touch the idea or sensation called *heat,* we do from thence conclude the sun to be the cause of heat. And in like manner perceiving the motion and collision of bodies to be attended with sound, we are inclined to think the latter an effect of the former.

(33) The ideas imprinted on the senses by the Author of Nature are called *real things:* and those excited in the imagination, being less regular, vivid and constant, are more properly termed *ideas,* or *images of things,* which they copy and represent. But then our sensations, be they never so vivid and distinct, are nevertheless *ideas,* that is, they exist in the mind, or are perceived by it, as truly as the ideas of its own framing. The ideas of sense are allowed to have more reality in them, that is, to be more strong, orderly, and coherent than the creatures of the mind; but this is no argument that they exist without the mind. They are also less dependent on the spirit or thinking substance which perceives them, in that they are excited by the will of another and more powerful spirit: yet still they are *ideas,* and certainly no *idea,* whether faint or strong, can exist otherwise than in a mind perceiving it.

(34) Before we proceed any farther, it is necessary to spend some

time in answering objections which may probably be made against the principles hitherto laid down. In doing of which, if I seem too prolix to those of quick apprehensions, I hope it may be pardoned, since all men do not equally apprehend things of this nature; and I am willing to be understood by everyone. First then, it will be objected that by the foregoing principles, all that is real and substantial in Nature is banished out of the world: and instead thereof a chimerical scheme of ideas takes place. All things that exist, exist only in the mind, that is, they are purely notional. What therefore becomes of the sun, moon, and stars? What must we think of houses, rivers, mountains, trees, stones; nay, even of our bodies? Are all these but so many chimeras and illusions on the fancy? To all which, and whatever else of the same sort may be objected, I answer, that by the principles premised, we are not deprived of any one thing in Nature. Whatever we see, feel, hear, or any wise conceive or understand, remains as secure as ever, and is as real as ever. There is a *rerum natura,* and the distinction between realities and chimeras retains its full force. This is evident from Sections 29, 30, and 33, where we have shown what is meant by *real things* in opposition to *chimeras,* or ideas of our own framing; but then they both equally exist in the mind, and in that sense are alike *ideas.*

* * * * * * * * * * * *

(37) It will be urged that thus much at least is true, to wit, that we take away all corporeal substances. To this my answer is, that if the word *substance* be taken in the vulgar sense, for a combination of sensible qualities, such as extension, solidity, weight, and the like: this we cannot be accused of taking away. But if it be taken in a philosophic sense, for the support of accidents or qualities without the mind: then indeed I acknowledge that we take it away, if one may be said to take away that which never had any existence, not even in the imagination.

* * * * * * * * * * * *

(86) From the principles we have laid down, it follows, human knowledge may naturally be reduced to two heads, that of *ideas,* and that of *spirits.* Of each of these I shall treat in order. And first as to ideas or unthinking things, our knowledge of these hath been

very much obscured and confounded, and we have been led into very dangerous errors, by supposing a twofold existence of the objects of sense, the one *intelligible*, or in the mind, the other *real* and without the mind: whereby unthinking things are thought to have a natural subsistence of their own, distinct from being perceived by spirits. This, which, if I mistake not, hath been shown to be a most groundless and absurd notion, is the very root of *scepticism;* for so long as men thought that real things subsisted without the mind, and that their knowledge was only so far forth *real* as it was conformable to *real things,* it follows, they could not be certain that they had any real knowledge at all. For how can it be known that the things which are perceived are conformable to those which are not perceived, or exist without the mind?

(87) Colour, figure, motion, extension, and the like, considered only as so many *sensations* in the mind, are perfectly known, there being nothing in them which is not perceived. But if they are looked on as notes or images, referred to *things* or *archetypes* existing without the mind, then are we involved all in *scepticism*. We see only the appearances, and not the real qualities of things. What may be the extension, figure, or motion of anything really and absolutely, or in itself, it is impossible for us to know, but only the proportion or the relation they bear to our senses. Things remaining the same, our ideas vary, and which of them, or even whether any of them at all represent the true quality really existing in the thing, it is out of our reach to determine. So that, for aught we know, all we see, hear, and feel, may be only phantom and vain chimera, and not at all agree with the real things existing in *rerum natura*. All this scepticism follows from our supposing a difference between *things* and *ideas,* and that the former have a subsistence without the mind, or unperceived. It were easy to dilate on this subject, and show how the arguments urged by *sceptics* in all ages depend on the supposition of external objects.

* • • • • • • • • • • • •

(145) From what hath been said, it is plain that we cannot know the existence of other spirits, otherwise than by their operations, or the ideas by them excited in us. I perceive several motions, changes, and combinations of ideas, that inform me there are certain particular agents like myself, which accompany them, and concur in

their production. Hence the knowledge I have of other spirits is not immediate as is the knowledge of my ideas; but depending on the intervention of ideas, by me referred to agents or spirits distinct from myself, as effects or concomitant signs.

(146) But though there be some things which convince us, human agents are concerned in producing them; yet it is evident to everyone, that those things which are called the works of Nature, that is, the far greater part of the ideas or sensations perceived by us, are not produced by, or dependent on the wills of men. There is therefore some other spirit that causes them, since it is repugnant that they should subsist by themselves. See Section 29. But if we attentively consider the constant regularity, order, and concatenation of natural things, the surprising magnificence, beauty, and perfection of the larger, and the exquisite contrivance of the smaller parts of the creation, together with the exact harmony and correspondence of the whole, but above all, the never enough admired laws of pain and pleasure, and the instincts or natural inclinations, appetites and passions of animals; I say if we consider all these things, and at the same time attend to the meaning and import of the attributes, one, eternal, infinitely wise, good, and perfect, we shall clearly perceive that they belong to the aforesaid spirit, *who works all in all,* and *by whom all things consist.*

(147) Hence it is evident, that God is known as certainly and immediately as any other mind or spirit whatsoever, distinct from ourselves. We may even assert, that the existence of God is far more evidently perceived than the existence of men; because the effects of Nature are infinitely more numerous and considerable than those ascribed to human agents. There is not any one mark that denotes a man, or effect produced by him, which doth not more strongly evince the being of that spirit who is the *Author of Nature.* For it is evident that in affecting other persons, the will of man hath no other object, than barely the motion of the limbs of his body; but that such a motion should be attended by or excite any idea in the mind of another, depends wholly on the will of the Creator. He alone it is who, *upholding all things by the Word of his Power,* maintains that intercourse between spirits whereby they are able to perceive the existence of each other. And yet this pure and clear light which enlightens every one is itself invisible.

THOMAS REID

A Common Sense Approach
to the Foundations
of Knowledge

One of the most important distinctions of our judgments is that some of them are intuitive, others grounded on argument.

It is not in our power to judge as we will. The judgment is carried along necessarily by the evidence, real or seeming, which appears to us at the time. But in propositions that are submitted to our judgment there is this great difference—some are of such a nature that a man of ripe understanding may apprehend them distinctly, and perfectly understand their meaning, without finding himself under any necessity of believing them to be true or false, probable or improbable. The judgment remains in suspense until it is inclined to one side or another by reasons or arguments.

But there are other propositions which are no sooner understood than they are believed. The judgment follows the apprehension of them necessarily, and both are equally the work of nature and the result of our original powers. There is no searching for evidence, no weighing of arguments; the proposition is not deduced or inferred from another; it has the light of truth in itself, and has no occasion to borrow it from another.

Propositions of the last kind, when they are used in matters of science, have commonly been called *axioms;* and on whatever occasion they are used, are called *first principles, principles of common sense, common notions, self-evident truths.* . . .

* From Thomas Reid, *Essays on the Intellectual Powers of Man,* 1785, Essay Six, Chap. 4 (with omissions).

What has been said, I think, is sufficient to distinguish first principles, or intuitive judgments, from those which may be ascribed to the power of reasoning; nor is it a just objection against this distinction that there may be some judgments concerning which we may be dubious to which class they ought to be referred. There is a real distinction between persons within the house and those that are without, yet it may be dubious to which the man belongs that stands upon the threshold.

The power of reasoning—that is, of drawing a conclusion from a chain of premises—may with some propriety be called an art. "All reasoning," says Mr. Locke, "is search and casting about, and requires pains and application." It resembles the power of walking, which is acquired by use and exercise. Nature prompts to it, and has given the power of acquiring it, but must be aided by frequent exercise before we are able to walk. After repeated efforts, much stumbling, and many falls, we learn to walk; and it is in a similar manner that we learn to reason.

But the power of judging in self-evident propositions, which are clearly understood, may be compared to the power of swallowing our food. It is purely natural, and therefore common to the learned and the unlearned, to the trained and the untrained. It requires ripeness of understanding and freedom from prejudice, but nothing else.

I take it for granted that there are self-evident principles. Nobody, I think, denies it. And if any man were so sceptical as to deny that there is any proposition that is self-evident, I see not how it would be possible to convince him by reasoning.

But yet there seems to be great difference of opinions among philosophers about first principles. What one takes to be self-evident, another labours to prove by arguments, and a third denies altogether.

. . . .

When in disputes one man maintains that to be a first principle which another denies, commonly both parties appeal to common sense, and so the matter rests. Now, is there no way of discussing this appeal? Is there no mark or criterion whereby first principles that are truly such may be distinguished from those that assume the character without a just title? I shall humbly offer in the following propositions what appears to me to be agreeable to truth in these matters, always ready to change my opinion upon conviction.

(1) *First,* I hold it to be certain, and even demonstrable, that all knowledge got by reasoning must be built upon first principles.

●   ●   ●   ●   ●   ●   ●   ●   ●   ●   ●   ●

When we examine in the way of analysis the evidence of any proposition, either we find it self-evident or it rests upon one or more propositions that support it. The same thing may be said of the propositions that support it, and of those that support them, as far back as we can go. But we cannot go back in this track to infinity. Where then must this analysis stop? It is evident that it must stop only when we come to propositions which support all that are built upon them, but are themselves supported by none— that is, to self-evident propositions.

Let us again consider a synthetical proof of any kind where we begin with the premises, and pursue a train of consequences until we come to the last conclusion or thing to be proved. Here we must begin either with self-evident propositions or with such as have been already proved. When the last is the case, the proof of the propositions thus assumed is a part of our proof, and the proof is deficient without it. Suppose then the deficiency supplied, and the proof completed, is it not evident that it must set out with self-evident propositions and that the whole evidence must rest upon them? So that it appears to be demonstrable that, without first principles, analytical reasoning could have no end, and synthetical reasoning could have no beginning; and that every conclusion got by reasoning must rest with its whole weight upon first principles, as the building does upon its foundation.

(2) A *second* proposition is, That some first principles yield conclusions that are certain, others such as are probable, in various degrees, from the highest probability to the lowest.

In just reasoning, the strength or weakness of the conclusion will always correspond to that of the principles on which it is grounded.

In a matter of testimony it is self-evident that the testimony of two is better than that of one, supposing them equal in character and in their means of knowledge, yet the simple testimony may be true and that which is preferred to it may be false.

When an experiment has succeeded in several trials, and the

circumstances have been marked with care, there is a self-evident probability of its succeeding in a new trial; but there is no certainty. The probability in some cases is much greater than in others, because in some cases it is much easier to observe all the circumstances that may have influence upon the event than in others. And it is possible that, after many experiments made with care, our expectation may be frustrated in a succeeding one by the variation of some circumstance that has not, or perhaps could not be observed.

Sir Isaac Newton has laid it down as a first principle in natural philosophy that a property which has been found in all bodies upon which we have had access to make experiments, and which has always been found in its quantity to be in exact proportion to the quantity of matter in every body, is to be held as a universal property of matter.

This principle, as far as I know, has never been called in question. The evidence we have, that all matter is divisible, movable, solid, and inert, is resolvable into this principle; and, if it be not true, we cannot have any rational conviction that all matter has those properties. From the same principle that great man has shown that we have reason to conclude that all bodies gravitate towards each other.

This principle, however, has not that kind of evidence which mathematical axioms have. It is not a necessary truth whose contrary is impossible; nor did Sir Isaac ever conceive it to be such. And if it should ever be found, by just experiments, that there is any part in the composition of some bodies which has not gravity, the fact, if duly ascertained, must be admitted as an exception to the general law of gravitation.

In games of chance it is a first principle that every side of a die has an equal chance to be turned up, and that in a lottery every ticket has an equal chance of being drawn out. From such first principles as these, which are the best we can have in such matters, we may deduce by demonstrative reasoning the precise degree of probability of every event in such games.

But the principles of all this accurate and profound reasoning can never yield a certain conclusion, it being impossible to supply a defect in the first principles by any accuracy in the reasoning that is grounded upon them. As water by its gravity can rise no higher n its course than the fountain, however artfully it be conducted, so no conclusion of reasoning can have a greater degree of evidence than the first principles from which it is drawn.

From these instances it is evident that as there are some first principles that yield conclusions of absolute certainty, so there are others that can only yield probable conclusions, and that the lowest degree of probability must be grounded on first principles as well as absolute certainty.

•   •   •   •   •   •   •   •   •   •   •

(4) A *fourth* proposition is, That nature hath not left us destitute of means whereby the candid and honest part of mankind may be brought to unanimity when they happen to differ about first principles.

•   •   •   •   •   •   •   •   •   •   •

It may be observed that although it is contrary to the nature of first principles to admit of direct or *apodictical* proof, yet there are certain ways of reasoning even about them by which those that are just and solid may be confirmed, and those that are false may be detected. It may here be proper to mention some of the topics from which we may reason in matters of this kind.

First, It is a good argument *ad hominem* if it can be shown that a first principle which a man rejects stands upon the same footing with others which he admits; for when this is the case, he must be guilty of an inconsistency who holds the one and rejects the other.

Secondly, A first principle may admit of a proof *ad absurdum.*

In this kind of proof, which is very common in mathematics, we suppose the contradictory proposition to be true. We trace the consequences of that supposition in a train of reasoning, and if we find any of its necessary consequences to be manifestly absurd, we conclude the supposition from which it followed to be false, and therefore its contradictory to be true.

Thirdly, I conceive that the consent of ages and nations, of the learned and unlearned, ought to have great authority with regard to first principles where every man is a competent judge.

Our ordinary conduct in life is built upon first principles as well as our speculations in philosophy, and every motive to action supposes some belief. When we find a general agreement among men in principles that concern human life, this must have great authority with every sober mind that loves truth.

· · · · · · · · · · · ·

Here perhaps it will be said, What has authority to do in matters of opinion? Is truth to be determined by most votes? Or is authority to be again raised out of its grave to tyrannise over mankind?

I am aware that in this age an advocate for authority has a very unfavourable plea, but I wish to give no more to authority than is its due.

Most justly do we honour the names of those benefactors to mankind who have contributed more or less to break the yoke of that authority which deprives men of the natural, the unalienable right of judging for themselves; but, while we indulge a just animosity against this authority and against all who would subject us to its tyranny, let us remember how common the folly is of going from one faulty extreme into the opposite.

Authority, though a very tyrannical mistress to private judgment, may yet on some occasions be a useful handmaid. This is all she is entitled to, and this is all I plead in her behalf.

The justice of this plea will appear by putting a case in a science in which, of all sciences, authority is acknowledged to have least weight.

Suppose a mathematician has made a discovery in that science which he thinks important, that he has put his demonstration in just order, and, after examining it with an attentive eye, has found no flaw in it, I would ask, Will there not be still in his breast some diffidence, some jealousy, lest the ardour of invention may have made him overlook some false step? This must be granted.

He commits his demonstration to the examination of a mathematical friend whom he esteems a competent judge, and waits with impatience the issue of his judgment. Here I would ask again whether the verdict of his friend, according as it is favourable or unfavourable, will not greatly increase or diminish his confidence in his own judgment. Most certainly it will, and it ought.

If the judgment of his friend agree with his own, especially if it be confirmed by two or three able judges, he rests secure of his discovery without further examination; but if it be unfavourable, he is brought back into a kind of suspense until the part that is suspected undergoes a new and a more rigorous examination.

•   •   •   •   •   •   •   •   •   •   •   •

In a matter of common sense every man is no less a competent judge than a mathematician is in a mathematical demonstration, and there must be a great presumption that the judgment of mankind in such a matter is the natural issue of those faculties which God hath given them. Such a judgment can be erroneous only when there is some cause of the error as general as the error is. When this can be shown to be the case, I acknowledge it ought to have its due weight. But to suppose a general deviation from truth among mankind in things self-evident, of which no cause can be assigned, is highly unreasonable.

Perhaps it may be thought impossible to collect the general opinion of men upon any point whatsoever; and, therefore, that this authority can serve us in no stead in examining first principles. But I apprehend that, in many cases, this is neither impossible nor difficult.

Who can doubt whether men have universally believed the existence of a material world? Who can doubt whether men have universally believed that every change that happens in nature must have a cause? Who can doubt whether men have universally believed, that there is a right and a wrong in human conduct; some things that merit blame, and others that are entitled to approbation?

The universality of these opinions, and of many such that might be named, is sufficiently evident, from the whole tenor of human conduct, as far as our acquaintance reaches, and from the history of all ages and nations of which we have any records.

There are other opinions that appear to be universal from what is common in the structure of all languages.

Language is the express image and picture of human thoughts, and from the picture we may draw some certain conclusions concerning the original.

We find in all languages the same parts of speech; we find nouns, substantive and adjective; verbs, active and passive, in their various tenses, numbers, and moods. Some rules of syntax are the same in all languages.

Now what is common in the structure of languages indicates a uniformity of opinion in those things upon which that structure is grounded.

The distinction between substances and the qualities belonging to them, between thought and the being that thinks, between thought and the objects of thought, is to be found in the structure of all languages. And, therefore, systems of philosophy which abolish those distinctions wage war with the common sense of mankind.

We are apt to imagine that those who formed languages were no metaphysicians; but the first principles of all sciences are the dictates of common sense, and lie open to all men, and every man who has considered the structure of language in a philosophical light will find infallible proofs that those who have framed it, and those who use it with understanding, have the power of making accurate distinctions and of forming general conceptions as well as philosophers. Nature has given those powers to all men, and they can use them when occasions require it, but they leave it to the philosophers to give names to them and to descant upon their nature. In like manner nature has given eyes to all men, and they can make good use of them; but the structure of the eye, and the theory of vision, is the business of philosophers.

Fourthly, Opinions that appear so early in the minds of men that they cannot be the effect of education or of false reasoning, have a good claim to be considered as first principles. Thus the belief we have that the persons about us are living and intelligent beings is a belief for which, perhaps, we can give some reason, when we are able to reason; but we had this belief before we could reason, and before we could learn it by instruction. It seems, therefore, to be an immediate effect of our constitution.

The *last topic* I shall mention is when an opinion is so necessary in the conduct of life that, without the belief of it, a man must be led into a thousand absurdities in practice; such an opinion, when we can give no other reason for it, may safely be taken for a first principle.

Thus I have endeavoured to show that, although first principles are not capable of direct proof, yet differences that may happen with regard to them among men of candour are not without remedy; that nature has not left us destitute of means by which we may discover errors of this kind; and that there are ways of reasoning, with regard to first principles, by which those that are truly such may be distinguished from vulgar errors or prejudices.

part three

CONTEMPORARY CHALLENGES TO THE PHILOSOPHIC TRADITION

KARL R. POPPER

Three Views Concerning
Human Knowledge

1. THE SCIENCE OF GALILEO AND ITS NEW BETRAYAL

Once upon a time there was a famous scientist whose name was
Galileo Galilei. He was tried by the Inquisition, and forced to
recant his teaching. This caused a great stir; and for well over two
hundred and fifty years the case continued to arouse indignation
and excitement—long after public opinion had won its victory, and
the Church had become tolerant of science.

But this is by now a very old story, and I fear it has lost its interest. For Galilean science has no enemies left, it seems: its life hereafter is secure. The victory won long ago was final, and all is quiet
on this front. So we take a detached view of the affair nowadays,
having learned at last to think historically, and to understand both
sides of a dispute. And nobody cares to listen to the bore who can't
forget an old grievance.

What, after all, was this old case about? It was about the status
of the Copernican "System of the World" which, besides other
things, explained the diurnal motion of the sun as only apparent,
and as due to the rotation of our own earth.[1] The Church was very

* Chapter 3 of *Conjectures and Refutations* by Karl R. Popper, © Karl R.
Popper, 1963, 1965, Basic Books, Inc., Publishers, New York. Reprinted also by
permission of Routledge & Kegan Paul Ltd.

[1] I emphasize here the diurnal as opposed to the annual motion of the sun
because it was the theory of the diurnal motion which clashed with *Joshua* 10,
12 f., and because the explanation of the diurnal motion of the sun by the motion of the earth will be one of my main examples in what follows. (This explanation is, of course, much older than Copernicus—older even than Aristarchus
—and it has been repeatedly rediscovered; for example by Oresme.)

ready to admit that the new system was simpler than the old one: that it was a more convenient *instrument* for astronomical calculations, and for predictions. And Pope Gregory's reform of the calendar made full practical use of it. There was no objection to Galileo's teaching the mathematical theory, so long as he made it clear that its value was *instrumental* only; that it was nothing but a "supposition," as Cardinal Bellarmino put it;[2] or a "mathematical hypothesis"—a kind of mathematical trick, "invented and assumed in order to abbreviate and ease the calculations." [3] In other words there were no objections so long as Galileo was ready to fall into line with Andreas Osiander who had said in his preface to Copernicus' *De revolutionibus*: "There is no need for these hypotheses to be true, or even to be at all like the truth; rather, one thing is sufficient for them—that they should yield calculations which agree with the observations."

Galileo himself, of course, was very ready to stress the superiority of the Copernican system as an *instrument of calculation*. But at the same time he conjectured, and even believed, that it was *a true description of the world*; and for him (as for the Church) this was by far the most important aspect of the matter. He had indeed some good reasons for believing in the truth of the theory. He had seen in his telescope that Jupiter and his moons formed a miniature

[2] ". . . Galileo will act prudently," wrote Cardinal Bellarmino (who had been one of the inquisitors in the case against Giordano Bruno) ". . . if he will speak hypothetically, *ex suppositione* . . . : to say that we give a better account of the appearances by supposing the earth to be moving, and the sun at rest, than we could if we used eccentrics and epicycles is to speak properly; there is no danger in that, and it is all that the mathematician requires." Cf. H. Grisar, *Galilei-studien*, 1882, App. ix. (Although this passage makes Bellarmino one of the founding fathers of the epistemology which Osiander had suggested some time before and which I am going to call "instrumentalism," Bellarmino unlike Berkeley was by no means a convinced instrumentalist himself, as other passages in this letter show. He merely saw in instrumentalism one of the possible ways dealing with inconvenient scientific hypotheses. The same remarks might well be true of Osiander. See also note 6, in section 2 below.)

[3] The quotation is from Bacon's criticism of Copernicus in the *Novum Organum*, ii, 36. In the next quotation (from *De revolutionibus*) I have translated the term *"verisimilis"* by "like the truth." It should certainly not be translated here by "probable"; for the whole point here is the question whether Copernicus' system is, or is not, similar in structure to the world; that is, whether it is truth-like. The questions of degree of certainty or probability does not arise. See also Chap. 10, especially Sections iii, x, and xiv; and *Addendum 6* in *Conjectures and Refutations*.

model of the Copernican solar system (according to which the planets were moons of the sun). Moreover, if Copernicus was right the inner planets (and they alone) should, when observed from the earth, show phases like the moon; and Galileo had seen in his telescope the phases of Venus.

The Church was unwilling to contemplate the truth of a New System of the World which seemed to contradict a passage in the Old Testament. But this was hardly its main reason. A deeper reason was clearly stated by Bishop Berkeley, about a hundred years later, in his criticism of Newton.

In Berkeley's time the Copernican System of the World had developed into Newton's Theory of gravity, and Berkeley saw in it a serious competitor to religion. He was convinced that a decline of religious faith and religious authority would result from the new science if its interpretation by the "freethinkers" was correct; for they saw in its success a proof of *the power of the human intellect, unaided by divine revelation, to uncover the secrets of our world*— the reality hidden behind its appearance.

This, Berkeley felt, was to misinterpret the new science. He analysed Newton's theory with complete candour and great philosophical acumen; and a critical survey of Newton's concepts convinced him that this theory could not possibly be anything but a "mathematical hypothesis," that is, a convenient *instrument* for the calculation and prediction of phenomena or appearances; that it could not possibly be taken as a true description of anything real.[4]

Berkeley's criticism was hardly noticed by the physicists; but it was taken up by philosophers, sceptical as well as religious. As a weapon it turned out to be a boomerang. In Hume's hands it became a threat to all belief—to all knowledge, whether human or revealed. In the hands of Kant, who firmly believed both in God and in the truth of Newtonian science, it developed into the doctrine that theoretical knowledge of God is impossible, and that Newtonian science must pay for the admission of its claim to truth by the renunciation of its claim to have discovered the real world behind the world of appearance: it was a true science of nature, but *nature* was precisely the world of mere phenomena, the world as it appeared to our assimilating minds. Later certain Pragmatists

[4] See also Chap. 6, of *Conjectures and Refutations*.

based their whole philosophy upon the view that the idea of "pure" knowledge was a mistake; that there could be no knowledge in any other sense but in the sense of *instrumental* knowledge; that knowledge was power, and that truth was usefulness.

Physicists (with a few brilliant exceptions[5]) kept aloof from all these philosophical debates, which remained completely inconclusive. Faithful to the tradition created by Galileo they devoted themselves to the search for truth, as he had understood it.

Or so they did until very recently. For all this is now past history. Today the view of physical science founded by Osiander, Cardinal Bellarmino, and Bishop Berkeley,[6] has won the battle without another shot being fired. Without any further debate over the philosophical issue, without producing any new argument, the *instrumentalist view* (as I shall call it) has become an accepted dogma. It may well now be called the "official view" of physical theory since it is accepted by most of our leading theorists of physics

[5] The most important of them are Mach, Kirchhoff, Hertz, Duhem, Poincaré, Bridgman, and Eddington—all instrumentalists in various ways.

[6] Duhem, in his famous series of papers, *Sōzein ta phainómena'* (*Ann. de philos. chrétienne*, anneé 79, tom 6, 1908, nos. 2 to 6), claimed for instrumentalism a much older and much more illustrious ancestry than is justified by the evidence. For the postulate that, with their hypotheses, scientists ought to "*account for the observed facts*," rather than "do violence to them by trying to squeeze or fit them into their theories" (Aristotle, *De Caelo*, 293a25; 296b6; 297a4; b24ff; *Met.* 1073b37, 107a1) has little to do with the instrumentalist thesis (that our theories can do *nothing but this*). Yet this postulate is essentially the same as that we ought to "*preserve the phenomena*" or "save" them ([*dia-*]*sōzein ta phainomena*). The phrase seems to be connected with the astronomical branch of the Platonic School tradition. (See especially the most interesting passage on Aristarchus in Plutarch's *De Facie in Orbe Lunae*, 923a; see also 933a for the "confirmation of the cause" by the phenomena, and Cherniss' note *a* on p. 168 of his edition of this work of Plutarch's; furthermore, Simplicius' commentaries on *De Caelo* where the phrase occurs *e.g.*, on pp. 497 1.21, 506 1.10, and 488 1.23 f, of Heiberg's edition, in commentaries on *De Caelo* 293a4 and 292b10.) We may well accept Simplicius' report that Eudoxus, under Plato's influence, in order to account for the observable phenomena of planetary motion, set himself the task of evolving an abstract geometrical system of rotating spheres *to which he did not attribute any physical reality*. (There seems to be some resemblance between this programme and that of the *Epinomis*, 990–91, where the study of abstract geometry —of the theory of the irrationals, 990d–991b—is described as a necessary preliminary to planetary theory; another such preliminary is the study of number, *i.e.*, the odd and the even, 990c.) Yet even this would not mean that either Plato or Eudoxus accepted an instrumentalist epistemology: they may have consciously (and wisely) confined themselves to a preliminary problem.

(although neither by Einstein nor by Schrödinger). And it has become part of the current teaching of physics.

2. THE ISSUE AT STAKE

All this looks like a great victory of philosophical critical thought over the naïve realism of the physicists. But I doubt whether this interpretation is right.

Few if any of the physicists who have now accepted the instrumentalist view of Cardinal Bellarmino and Bishop Berkeley realize that they have accepted a philosophical theory. Nor do they realize that they have broken with the Galilean tradition. On the contrary, most of them think that they have kept clear of philosophy; and most of them no longer care anyway. What they now care about, as physicists, is (a) *mastery of the mathematical formalism*, that is, of the instrument, and (b) *its applications;* and they care for nothing else. And they think that by thus excluding everything else they have finally got rid of all philosophical nonsense. This very attitude of being tough and not standing any nonsense prevents them from considering seriously the philosophical arguments for and against the Galilean view of science (though they will no doubt have heard of Mach[7]). Thus the victory of the instrumentalist philosophy is hardly due to the soundness of its arguments.

How then did it come about? As far as I can see, through the coincidence of two factors, (a) difficulties in the interpretation of the formalism of the Quantum Theory, and (b) the spectacular practical success of its applications.

(a) In 1927 Niels Bohr, one of the greatest thinkers in the field of atomic physics, introduced the so-called *principle of complementarity* into atomic physics, which amounted to a "renunciation" of the attempt to interpret atomic theory as a description of anything. Bohr pointed out that we could avoid certain contradictions (which threatened to arise between the formalism and its various interpretations) only by reminding ourselves that the formalism as such was self-consistent, and that each single case of its application

---

[7] But they seem to have forgotten that Mach was led by his instrumentalism to fight against atomic theory—a typical example of *the obscurantism of instrumentalism* which is the topic of section 5 below.

(or each kind of case) remained consistent with it. The contradictions only arose through the attempt to comprise within *one* interpretation the formalism together with more than one case, or kind of case, of its experimental application. But, as Bohr pointed out, any two of these conflicting applications were physically incapable of ever being combined in one experiment. Thus the result of *every single* experiment was consistent with the theory, and unambiguously laid down by it. This, he said, was all we could get. The claim to get more, and even the hope of ever getting more, we must renounce; physics remains consistent only if we do not try to interpret, or to understand, its theories beyond (*a*) mastering the formalism, and (*b*) relating them to each of their actually realizable cases of application separately.[8]

Thus the instrumentalist philosophy was used here *ad hoc* in order to provide an escape for the theory from certain contradictions by which it was threatened. It was used in a defensive mood to rescue the existing theory; and the principle of complementarity has (I believe for this reason) remained completely sterile within physics. In twenty-seven years it has produced nothing except some philosophical discussions, and some arguments for the confounding of critics (especially Einstein).

I do not believe that physicists would have accepted such an *ad hoc* principle had they understood that it was *ad hoc*, or that it was a philosophical principle—part of Bellarmino's and Berkeley's instrumentalist philosophy of physics. But they remembered Bohr's earlier and extremely fruitful 'principle of correspondence' and hoped (in vain) for similar results.

(*b*) Instead of results due to the principle of complementarity other and more practical results of atomic theory were obtained, some of them with a big bang. No doubt physicists were perfectly right in interpreting these successful applications as corroborating their theories. But strangely enough they took them as confirming the instrumentalist creed.

Now this was an obvious mistake. The instrumentalist view asserts

[8] I have explained Bohr's "Principle of Complementarity" as I understand it after many years of effort. No doubt I shall be told that my formulation of it is unsatisfactory. But if so I am in good company; for Einstein refers to it as "Bohr's principle of complementarity, a sharp formulation of which . . . I have been unable to attain despite much effort which I have expended on it." Cf. *Albert Einstein: Philosopher-Scientist,* ed. by P. A. Schlipp, 1949, p. 674.

that theories are *nothing but* instruments, while the Galilean view was that they are not only instruments but also—and mainly— descriptions of the world, or of certain aspects of the world. It is clear that in this disagreement even a proof showing that theories are instruments (assuming it possible to "prove" such a thing) could not seriously be claimed to support either of the two parties to the debate, since both were agreed on this point.

If I am right, or even roughly right, in my account of the situation, then philosophers, even instrumentalist philosophers, have no reason to take pride in their victory. On the contrary, they should examine their arguments again. For at least in the eyes of those who like myself do not accept the instrumentalist view, there is much at stake in this issue.

The issue, as I see it, is this.

One of the most important ingredients of our western civilization is what I may call the "rationalist tradition" which we have inherited from the Greeks. It is the tradition of critical discussion— not for its own sake, but in the interests of the search for truth. Greek science, like Greek philosophy, was one of the products of this tradition,[9] and of the urge to understand the world in which we live; and the tradition founded by Galileo was its renaissance.

Within this rationalist tradition science is valued, admittedly, for its practical achievements; but it is even more highly valued for its informative content, and for its ability to free our minds from old beliefs, old prejudices, and old certainties, and to offer us in their stead new conjectures and daring hypotheses. Science is valued for its liberalizing influence—as one of the greatest of the forces that make for human freedom.

According to the view of science which I am trying to defend here, this is due to the fact that scientists have dared (since Thales, Democritus, Plato's *Timaeus,* and Aristarchus) to create myths, or conjectures, or theories, which are in striking contrast to the everyday world of common experience, yet able to explain some aspects of this world of common experience. Galileo pays homage to Aristarchus and Copernicus precisely because they dared to go beyond this known world of our senses: "I cannot," he writes,[10] express

[9] See Chap. 4 of *Conjectures and Refutations.*
[10] Salviati says so several times, with hardly a verbal variation, on the Third Day of *The Two Principal Systems.*

strongly enough my unbounded admiration for the greatness of mind of these men who conceived [the heliocentric system] and held it to be true . . . , in violent opposition to the evidence of their own senses. . . ." This is Galileo's testimony to the liberalizing force of science. Such theories would be important even if they were no more than exercises for our imagination. But they are more than this, as can be seen from the fact that we submit them to severe tests by trying to deduce from them some of the regularities of the known world of common experience, that is, by trying to *explain* these regularities. And these attempts to *explain the known by the unknown* (as I have described them elsewhere[11]) have immeasurably extended the realm of the known. They have added to the facts of our everyday world the invisible air, the antipodes, the circulation of the blood, the worlds of the telescope and the microscope, of electricity, and of tracer atoms showing us in detail the movements of matter within living bodies. All these things are far from being mere instruments: they are witness to the intellectual conquest of our world by our minds.

But there is another way of looking at these matters. For some, science is still nothing but glorified plumbing, glorified gadget-making—"mechanics"; very useful, but a danger to true culture, threatening us with the domination of the near-illiterate (of Shakespeare's "mechanicals"). It should never be mentioned in the same breath as literature or the arts or philosophy. Its professed discoveries are mere mechanical inventions, its theories are instruments—gadgets again, or perhaps supergadgets. It cannot and does not reveal to us new worlds behind our everyday world of appearance; for the physical world is just surface: it has no depth. *The world is just what it appears to be. Only the scientific theories are not what they appear to be.* A scientific theory neither explains nor describes the world; it is nothing but an instrument.

I do not present this as a complete picture of modern instrumentalism, although it is a fair sketch, I think, of part of its original philosophical background. Today a much more important part of it is, I am well aware, the rise and self-assertion of the modern

[11] See the App., point (10) to Chap. 1, and the penultimate paragraph of Chap. 6 of *Conjectures and Refutations*.

"mechanic" or engineer.[12] Still, I believe that the issue should be seen to lie between a critical and adventurous rationalism—the spirit of discovery—and a narrow and defensive creed according to which we cannot and need not learn or understand more about our world than we know already. A creed, moreover, which is incompatible with the appreciation of science as one of the greatest achievements of the human spirit.

Such are the reasons why I shall try, in this paper, to uphold at least part of the Galilean view of science against the instrumentalist view. But I cannot uphold all of it. There is a part of it which I believe the instrumentalists were right to attack. I mean the view that in science we can aim at, and obtain, *an ultimate explanation by essences.* It is in its opposition to this Aristotelian view (which I have called [13] "essentialism") that the strength and the philosophical interest of instrumentalism lies. Thus I shall have to discuss and criticize two views of human knowledge—*essentialism* and *instrumentalism.* And I shall oppose to them what I shall call *the third view*—what remains of Galileo's view after the elimination of essentialism, or more precisely, after allowance has been made for what was justified in the instrumentalist attack.

3. THE FIRST VIEW: ULTIMATE EXPLANATION BY ESSENCES

Essentialism, the first of the three views of scientific theory to be discussed, is part of the Galilean philosophy of science. Within this philosophy three elements or doctrines which concern us here may be distinguished. Essentialism (our "first view") is that part of the Galilean philosophy which I do not wish to uphold. It consists of a combination of the doctrines (two) and (three). These are the three doctrines:

(1) *The scientist aims at finding a true theory or description of*

---

[12] The realization that natural science is not indubitable *epistēmē (scientia)* has led to the view that it is *technē* (technique, art, technology); but the proper view, I believe, is that it consists of *doxai (opinions, conjectures),* controlled by critical discussion as well as by experimental *technē.* Cf. Chap. 20, of *Conjectures and Refutations.*

[13] See section 10 of my *Poverty of Historicism,* and my *Open Society and its Enemies,* Vol. I, Chap. 3, Section vi, and Vol. II, Chap. 11, Sections i and ii.

the world (and especially of its regularities or "laws"), *which shall also be an explanation of the observable facts.* (This means that a description of these facts must be deducible from the theory in conjunction with certain statements, the so-called "initial conditions.")

This is a doctrine I wish to uphold. It is to form part of our "third view."

(2) *The scientist can succeed in finally establishing the truth of such theories beyond all reasonable doubt.*

This second doctrine, I think, needs correction. All the scientist can do, in my opinion, is to test his theories, and to eliminate all those that do not stand up to the most severe tests he can design. But he can never be quite sure whether new tests (or even a new theoretical discussion) may not lead him to modify, or to discard, his theory. In this sense all theories are, and remain hypotheses: they are conjecture (*doxa*) as opposed to indubitable knowledge (*epistēmē*).

(3) *The best, the truly scientific theories, describe the "essences" or the "essential natures" of things—the realities which lie behind the appearances.* Such theories are neither in need nor susceptible of further explanation: they are *ultimate explanations*, and to find them is the ultimate aim of the scientist.

This third doctrine (in connection with the second) is the one I have called "essentialism." I believe that like the second doctrine it is mistaken.

Now what the instrumentalist philosophers of science, from Berkeley to Mach, Duhem, and Poincaré, have in common is this. They all assert that explanation is not an aim of physical science, since physical science cannot discover "the hidden essences of things." The argument shows that what they have in mind is what I call *ultimate* explanation.[14] Some of them, such as Mach and Berkeley, hold this view because they do not believe that there is such a thing as an essence of anything physical: Mach, because he does not believe in essences at all; Berkeley, because he believes only in spiritual

[14] The issue has been confused at times by the fact that the instrumentalist criticism of (ultimate) explanation was expressed by some with the help of the formula: the aim of science is *description rather than explanation.* But what was here meant by "description" was the description *of the ordinary empirical world*; and what the formula expressed, indirectly, was that those theories which do not describe *in this sense* do not explain either, but are nothing but convenient instruments to help us in the description of ordinary phenomena.

essences, and thinks that the only essential explanation of the world is God. Duhem seems to think (on lines reminiscent of Kant[15]) that there are essences but that they are undiscoverable by human science (though we may, somehow, move towards them); like Berkeley he thinks that they can be revealed by religion. But all these philosophers agree that (ultimate) scientific explanation is impossible. And from the absence of a hidden essence which scientific theories could describe they conclude that these theories (which clearly do not describe our ordinary world of common experience) describe nothing at all. Thus they are mere instruments.[16] And what may appear as the growth of theoretical knowledge is merely the improvement of instruments.

The instrumentalist philosophers therefore reject the third doctrine, that is, the doctrine of essences. (I reject it too, but for somewhat different reasons.) At the same time they reject, and are bound to reject, the second doctrine; for if a theory is an instrument, then it cannot be true (but only convenient, simple, economical, powerful, *etc.*). They even frequently call the theories "hypotheses"; but they do not, of course, mean by this what I mean: that a theory is *conjectured to be true*, that it is a descriptive though possibly a false statement; although they do mean to say that theories are uncertain: "And as to the usefulness of hypotheses," Osiander writes (at the end of his preface), "nobody should expect anything certain to emerge from astronomy, for nothing of the kind can ever come out of it." Now I fully agree that there is no certainty about theories (which may always be refuted); and I even agree that they are instruments, although I do not agree that this is the reason why there can be no certainty about theories. (The correct reason, I believe, is simply that our tests can never be exhaustive.) There is thus a considerable amount of agreement between my instrumentalist opponents and myself over the second and third doctrines. But over the first doctrine there is complete disagreement.

To this disagreement I shall return later. In the present section I shall try to criticize (three), the essentialist doctrine of science, on lines somewhat different from the arguments of the instrumentalism which I cannot accept. For its argument that there can be no

---

[15] Cf. Kant's letter to Reinhold, 12.5.1789, in which the "real essence" or "nature" of a thing (*e.g.*, of matter) is said to be inaccessible to human knowledge.

[16] See Chap. 6 of *Conjectures and Refutations*.

"hidden essences" is based upon its conviction that *there can be nothing hidden* (or that if anything is hidden it can be only known by divine revelation). From what I said in the last section it will be clear that I cannot accept an argument that leads to the rejection of the claim of science to have discovered the rotation of the earth, or atomic nuclei, or cosmic radiation, or the "radio stars."

I therefore readily concede to essentialism that much is hidden from us, and that much of what is hidden may be discovered. (I disagree profoundly with the spirit of Wittgenstein's dictum, "The riddle does not exist.") And I do not even intend to criticize those who try to understand the "essence of the world." The essentialist doctrine I am contesting is solely *the doctrine that science aims at ultimate explanation;* that is to say, an explanation which (essentially, or by its very nature) cannot be further explained, and which is in no need of any further explanation.

Thus my criticism of essentialism does not aim at establishing the nonexistence of essences; it merely aims at showing the obscurantist character of the role played by the idea of essences in the Galilean philosophy of science (down to Maxwell, who was inclined to believe in them but whose work destroyed this belief). In other words my criticism tries to show that whether essences exist or not the belief in them does not help us in any way and indeed is likely to hamper us; so that there is no reason why the scientist should *assume* their existence.[17]

---

[17] This criticism of mine is thus frankly utilitarian, and it might be described as instrumentalist; but I am concerned here with a *problem of method* which is always a problem of the fitness of means to ends.

My attacks upon *essentialism*—i.e., upon the *doctrine of ultimate explanation* —have sometimes been countered by the remark that I myself operate (perhaps unconsciously) with the idea of an *essence of science* (or an *essence of human knowledge*), so that my argument, if made explicit, would run: "It is of the essence or of the nature of human science (or human knowledge) that we cannot know, or search for, such things as essences or natures." I have however answered, by implication, this particular objection at some length in *The Logic of Scientific Discovery* (sections 9 and 10, "The Naturalist View of Method") and I did so before it was ever raised—in fact before I ever came to describe, and to attack, essentialism. Moreover, one might adopt the view that certain *things of our own making*—such as clocks—may well be said to have "essences," *viz.,* their "purposes" (and what makes them serve these "purposes"). And science, as a human, purposeful activity (or a method), *might* therefore be claimed by some to have an "essence," even if they deny that natural objects have essences. (This denial is not, however, implied in my criticism of essentialism.)

This, I think, can be best shown with the help of a simple example —*the Newtonian theory of gravity.*

The essentialist interpretation of Newtonian theory is due to Roger Cotes.[18] According to him Newton discovered that every particle of matter was endowed with *gravity*, that is, with an inherent power or force to attract other matter. It was also endowed with *inertia*—an inherent power to resist a change in its state of motion (or to retain the direction and velocity of its motion). Since both gravity and inertia inhere in each particle of matter it follows that both must be strictly proportional to the amount of matter in a body, and therefore to each other; hence the law of proportionality of inert and gravitating mass. Since gravity radiates from each particle we obtain the square law of attraction. In other words, Newton's laws of motion simply describe in mathematical language the state of affairs due to the inherent properties of matter: they describe the *essential nature of matter.*

Since Newton's theory described in this way the essential nature of matter, he could explain the behaviour of matter with its help, by mathematical deduction. But Newton's theory, in its turn, is neither capable of, nor in need of, further explanation, according to Cotes—at least not within physics. (The only possible further explanation was that God has endowed matter with these essential properties.[19])

This essentialist view of Newton's theory was on the whole the accepted view until the last decades of the nineteenth century. That it was obscurantist is clear: *it prevented fruitful questions from being raised*, such as, "What is the cause of gravity?" or more fully, "Can we perhaps explain gravity by deducing Newton's theory, or a good approximation of it, from a more general theory (which should be independently testable)?"

Now it is illuminating to see that Newton himself had not considered *gravity* as an essential property of matter (although he considered *inertia* to be essential, and also, with Descartes, *extension.*) It appears that he had taken over from Descartes the view that the essence of a thing must be a true or absolute property of the thing (i.e., a property which does not depend on the existence of other

---

[18] R. Cotes' Preface to the second edition of Newton's *Principia.*

[19] There is an essentialist theory of Time and Space (similar to this theory of matter) which is due to Newton himself.

things) such as extension, or the power to resist a change in its state of motion, and not a relational property, that is, a property which, like gravity, determines the relations (interactions in space) between one body and other bodies. Accordingly, he strongly felt the incompleteness of this theory, and the need to explain gravity. "That gravity," he wrote,[20] "should be innate, inherent, and essential to matter, so that one body may act upon another at a distance . . . is to me so great an absurdity that I believe no man who has in philosophical matters a competent faculty of thinking can ever fall into it."

It is interesting to see that Newton condemned here, in anticipation, the bulk of his followers. To them, one is tempted to remark, the properties of which they had learned in school appeared to be essential (and even self-evident), although to Newton, with his Cartesian background, the same properties had appeared to be in need of explanation (and indeed to be almost paradoxical).

Yet Newton himself was an essentialist. He had tried hard to find an acceptable ultimate explanation of gravity by trying to deduce the square law from the assumption of a mechanical push—the only kind of causal action which Descartes had permitted, since only push could be explained by the essential property of all bodies, extension.[21] But he failed. Had he succeeded we can be certain that he would have thought that his problem was finally solved—that he had found the ultimate explanation of gravity.[22] But here he would have been wrong. The question, "Why can bodies push one an-

[20] Letter to Richard Bentley, 25th February 1692–93 (*i.e.*, 1693); cf. also the letter of 17th January.

[21] This Cartesian theory of causality is of decisive importance for the whole history of physics. It led to the principle of action by contact, and later to the more abstract "principle of *action at vanishing distances*" (as I may call it), of an action propagated from each point to its immediate vicinity; *i.e.*, to the principle of differential equations.

[22] Newton was an essentialist for whom gravity was not acceptable as an ultimate explanation, but he was unsuccessful in his attempts to explain it further mathematically. Descartes, in such a situation, would have postulated the existence of some push-mechanism: he would have proposed what he called a "hypothesis." But Newton, with a critical allusion to Descartes, said that, in this situation, he was not going to invent arbitrary *ad hoc* hypotheses (*hypotheses non fingo*). Of course, he could not but operate constantly with hypotheses (*e.g.*, with an atomistic theory of light "rays"); but this saying of his has been interpreted as an authoritative criticism of the method of hypotheses, or (by Duhem) as a declaration of his instrumentalism.

other?" *can* be asked (as Leibniz first saw), and it is even an extremely fruitful question. (We now believe that they push one another because of certain repulsive electric forces.) But Cartesian and Newtonian essentialism, especially if Newton had been successful in his attempted explanation of gravity, might have prevented this question from ever being raised.

These examples, I think, make it clear that the belief in essences (whether true or false) is liable to create obstacles to thought—to the posing of new and fruitful problems. Moreover, it cannot be part of science (for even if we should, by a lucky chance, hit upon a theory describing essences, we could never be sure of it). But a creed which is likely to lead to obscurantism is certainly not one of those extra-scientific beliefs (such as a faith in the power of critical discussion) which a scientist need accept.

This concludes my criticism of essentialism.

4. THE SECOND VIEW: THEORIES AS INSTRUMENTS

The instrumentalist view has great attractions. It is modest, and it is very simple, especially if compared with essentialism.

According to essentialism we must distinguish between (i) the universe of essential reality, (ii) the universe of observable phenomena, and (iii) the universe of descriptive language or of symbolic representation. I will take each of these to be represented by a square.

The function of a theory may here be described as follows.

a, b are phenomena; *A, B* are the corresponding realities behind these appearances; and α, β the descriptions or symbolic representations of these realities. *E* are the essential properties of *A, B*, and ϵ is the theory describing *E*. Now from ϵ and α we can deduce β; this means that we can explain, with the help of our theory, why *a* leads to, or is the cause of, *b*.

A representation of instrumentalism can be obtained from this schema simply by omitting (i), that is, the universe of the realities behind the various appearances. α then directly describes *a*, and β directly describes *b*; and ϵ describes nothing—it is merely an instrument which helps us to deduce β from α. (This may be expressed by saying, as Schlick did, following Wittgenstein—that a universal law or a theory is not a proper statement but rather "a rule, or a

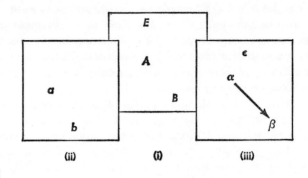

FIG. 1

set of instructions, for the derivation of singular statements from other singular statements." [23]

This is the instrumentalist view. In order to understand it better we may again take Newtonian dynamics as an example. a and b may be taken to be two positions of two spots of light (or two positions of the planet Mars); α and β are the corresponding formulae of the formalism; and ϵ is the theory strengthened by a general description of the solar system (or by a "model" of the solar system). Nothing corresponds to ϵ in the world (in the universe ii): there simply are no such things as attractive forces, for example. Newtonian forces are not entities which determine the acceleration of bodies: they are nothing but mathematical tools whose function is to allow us to deduce β from α.

No doubt we have here an attractive simplification, a radical application of Ockham's razor. But although this simplicity has converted many to instrumentalism (for example Mach) it is by no means the strongest argument in its favour.

Berkeley's strongest argument for instrumentalism was based upon his nominalistic philosophy of language. According to this philosophy the expression "force of attraction" must be a meaningless

[23] For an analysis and criticism of this view see my *The Logic of Scientific Discovery* especially note 7 to section 4, and my *Open Society*, note 51 to Chap. 11. The idea that universal statements may function in this way can be found in Mill's *Logic*, Book II, Chap. iii, p. 3: "All inference is from particulars to particulars." See also G. Ryle, *The Concept of Mind* (1949), *Chap.* v, pp. 121 ff., for a more careful and critical formulation of the same view.

expression, since forces of attraction can never be observed. What can be observed are movements, not their hidden alleged "causes." This is sufficient, on Berkeley's view of language, to show that Newton's theory cannot have any informative or descriptive content.

Now this argument of Berkeley's may perhaps be criticized because of the intolerably narrow theory of meaning which it implies. For if consistently applied it amounts to the thesis that all dispositional words are without meaning. Not only would Newtonian "attractive forces" be without meaning, but also such ordinary dispositional words and expressions as "breakable" (as opposed to "broken"), or "capable of conducting electricity" (as opposed to "conducting electricity"). These are not names of anything observable, and they would therefore have to be treated on a par with Newtonian forces. But it would be awkward to classify all these expressions as meaningless, and *from the point of view of instrumentalism* it is quite unnecessary to do so: all that is needed is an analysis of the meaning of dispositional terms and dispositional statements. This will reveal that they have meaning. But from the point of view of instrumentalism they do not have a descriptive meaning (like nondispositional terms and statements). Their function is not to report events, or occurrences, or "incidents," in the world, or to describe facts. Rather, their meaning exhausts itself in the permission or licence which they give us to draw inferences or to argue from some matters of fact to other matters of fact. Nondispositional statements which describe observable matters of fact ("this leg is broken") have cash value, as it were; dispositional statements, to which belong the laws of science, are not like cash, but rather like legal *"instruments"* creating rights to cash.

One need only proceed one step further in the same direction, it appears, in order to arrive at an instrumentalist argument which it is extremely difficult, if not impossible, to criticize; for our whole question—whether science is descriptive or instrumental—is here exposed as a pseudo-problem.[24]

The step in question consists, simply, in not only allowing mean-

---

[24] I have not so far encountered in the literature this particular form of the instrumentalist argument; but if we remember the parallelism between problems concerning the *meaning* of an expression and problems concerning the *truth* of a statement (see for example the table in the Introduction to *Conjectures and Refutations,* Section xii), we see that this argument closely corresponds to William James' definition of "truth" as "usefulness."

ing—an instrumental meaning—to dispositional terms, but also a kind of *descriptive meaning*. Dispositional words such as "break-able," it may be said, certainly describe something; for to say of a thing that it is breakable is to describe it as a thing that can be broken. But to say of a thing that it is breakable, or soluble, is to describe it in a different way, and by a different method, from saying that it is broken or dissolved; otherwise we should not use the suffix "able." The difference is just this—that we describe, by using dispositional words, what may happen to a thing (in certain circumstances). Accordingly, dispositional descriptions *are* descriptions, but they have nevertheless a purely instrumental function. In their case, knowledge *is* power (the power to foresee). When Galileo said of the earth "and yet, it moves," then he uttered, no doubt, a descriptive statement. But the function or meaning of this statement turns out nevertheless to be purely instrumental: it exhausts itself in the help it renders in deducing certain nondispositional statements.

Thus the attempt to show that theories have a descriptive meaning *besides* their instrumental meaning is misconceived, according to this argument; and the whole problem—the issue between Galileo and the Church—turns out to be a pseudo-problem.

In support of the view that Galileo suffered for the sake of a pseudoproblem it has been asserted that in the light of a logically more advanced system of physics Galileo's problem has in fact dissolved into nothing. Einstein's general principle, one often hears, makes it quite clear that it is meaningless to speak of absolute motion, even in the case of rotation; for we can freely choose whatever system we wish to be (relatively) at rest. Thus Galileo's problem vanishes. Moreover, it vanishes precisely for the reasons given above. Astronomical knowledge can be nothing but knowledge of how the stars behave; thus it cannot be anything but the power to describe and predict our observations; and since these must be independent of our free choice of a coordinate system, we now see more clearly why Galileo's problem could not possibly be real.

I shall not criticize instrumentalism in this section, or reply to its arguments, except the very last one—the argument from general relativity. This argument is based on a mistake. From the point of view of general relativity, there is very good sense—even an absolute sense—in saying that the earth rotates: *it rotates in precisely that sense in which a bicycle wheel rotates*. It rotates, that is to say, with respect to *any* chosen local inertial system. Indeed relativity describes the solar system in such a way that from this description we can deduce that *any* observer situated on *any* sufficiently distant freely moving physical body (such as our moon, or another planet, or a star outside the system) would see the earth rotating, and could deduce, from this observation, that for its inhabitants there would be an apparent diurnal motion of the sun. But it is clear that this is precisely the sense of the words "it moves" which was at issue; for part of the issue was whether the solar system was a system like that of Jupiter and his moons, only bigger; and whether it would look like this system, if seen from outside. On all these questions Einstein unambiguously supports Galileo.

My argument should not be interpreted as an admission that the whole question can be reduced to one of observations, or of possible observations. Admittedly both Galileo and Einstein intend, among other things, to deduce what an observer, or a possible observer, would see. But this is not their main problem. Both investigate physical systems and their movements. It is only the instrumentalist philosopher who asserts that what they discussed, or "really meant" to discuss, were not physical systems but *only* the results of possible observations; and that their so-called "physical systems," which *appeared* to be their objects of study, were *in reality* only instruments for predicting observations.

5. CRITICISM OF THE INSTRUMENTALIST VIEW

Berkeley's argument, we have seen, depends upon the adoption of a certain philosophy of language, convincing perhaps at first, but not necessarily true. Moreover, it hinges on the *problem of meaning*,[25] notorious for its vagueness and hardly offering hope of a solution. The position becomes even more hopeless if we consider some more recent development of Berkeley's arguments, as sketched in the preceding section. I shall try, therefore, to force a clear decision on our problem by a different approach—by way of an analysis of science rather than an analysis of language.

My proposed criticism of the instrumentalist view of scientific theories can be summarized as follows.

---

[25] For this problem see my two books mentioned here in note 23, and Chaps. 1, 11, 13 and 14 of *Conjectures and Refutations*.

Instrumentalism can be formulated as the thesis that scientific theories—the theories of the so-called "pure" sciences—are nothing but computation rules (or inference rules); of the same character, fundamentally, as the computation rules of the so-called "applied" sciences. (One might even formulate it as the thesis that "pure" science is a misnomer, and that all science is "applied.")

Now my reply to instrumentalism consists in showing that there are profound differences between "pure" theories and technological computation rules, and that instrumentalism can give a perfect description of these rules but is quite unable to account for the difference between them and the theories. Thus instrumentalism collapses.

The analysis of the many functional differences between computation rules (for navigation, say) and scientific theories (such as Newton's) is a very interesting task, but a short list of results must suffice here. The logical relations which may hold between theories and computation rules are not symmetrical; and they are different from those which may hold between various theories, and also from those which may hold between various computation rules. The way in which computation rules are *tried out* is different from the way in which theories are *tested*; and the skill which the application of computation rules demands is quite different from that needed for their (theoretical) discussion, and for the (theoretical) determination of the limits of their applicability. These are only a few hints, but they may be enough to indicate the direction and the force of the argument.

I am now going to explain one of these points a little more fully, because it gives rise to an argument somewhat similar to the one I have used against essentialism. What I wish to discuss is the fact that theories are tested by *attempts to refute them* (attempts from which we learn a great deal), while there is nothing strictly corresponding to this in the case of technological rules of computation or calculation.

A theory is tested not merely by applying it, or by trying it out, but by applying it to very special cases—cases for which it yields results different from those we should have expected without that theory, or in the light of other theories. In other words we try to select for our tests those crucial cases in which we should expect the theory to fail if it is not true. Such cases are "crucial" in Bacon's sense; they indicate the crossroads between *two* (or more) theories. For to say that without the theory in question we should have expected a different result implies that our expectation was the result of some other (perhaps an older) theory, however dimly we may have been aware of this fact. But while Bacon believed that a crucial experiment may establish or verify a theory, we shall have to say that it can at most refute or falsify a theory.[26] It is an attempt to refute it; and if it does not succeed in refuting the theory in question —if, rather, the theory is successful with its unexpected prediction —then we say that it is corroborated by the experiment. (It is the better corroborated [27] the less expected, or the less probable, the result of the experiment has been.)

Against the view here developed one might be tempted to object (following Duhem[28]) that in every test it is not only the theory under investigation which is involved, but also the whole system of our theories and assumptions—in fact, more or less the whole of our knowledge—so that we can never be certain which of all these assumptions is refuted. But this criticism overlooks the fact that if we take each of the two theories (between which the crucial experiment is to decide) *together* with all this background knowledge, as indeed we must, then we decide between two systems which differ *only* over the two theories which are at stake. It further overlooks the fact that we do not assert the refutation of the theory as such, but of the theory *together* with that background knowledge; parts of which, if other crucial experiments can be designed, may indeed one day be rejected as responsible for the failure. (Thus we may even characterize a *theory under investigation* as that part of a vast system for which we have, if vaguely, an alternative in mind, and for which we try to design crucial tests.)

Now nothing sufficiently similar to such tests exists in the case of instruments or rules of computation. An instrument may break

[26] Duhem, in his famous criticism of crucial experiments (in his *Aim and Structure of Physical Theory*), succeeds in showing that crucial experiments can never *establish* a theory. He fails to show that they cannot *refute* it.

[27] The degree of corroboration will therefore increase with the improbability (or the content) of the corroborating cases. See my "Degree of Confirmation," *Brit. Jour. Phil. Sci.*, 5, pp. 143 ff., now among the new appendices of my *The Logic of Scientific Discovery* and Chap. 10 (including the *Addenda*) of *Conjectures and Refutations.*

[28] See note 26.

down, to be sure, or it may become outmoded. But it hardly makes sense to say that we submit an instrument to the severest tests we can design in order to reject it if it does not stand up to them: every air frame, for example, can be "tested to destruction," but this severe test is undertaken not in order to reject every frame when it is destroyed but to obtain information about the frame (*i.e.*, to test a theory about it), so that it may be used *within the limits of its applicability* (or safety).

For instrumental purposes of practical application a theory may continue to be used *even after its refutation,* within the limits of its applicability: an astronomer who believes that Newton's theory has turned out to be false will not hesitate to apply its formalism within the limits of its applicability.

We may sometimes be disappointed to find that the range of applicability of an instrument is smaller than we expected at first; but this does not make us discard the instrument *qua* instrument—whether it is a theory or anything else. On the other hand a disappointment of this kind means that we have obtained new *information* through refuting a *theory*—that theory which implied that the instrument was applicable over a wider range.

Instruments, even theories *in so far as they are instruments,* cannot be refuted, as we have seen. The instrumentalist interpretation will therefore be unable to account for real tests, which are attempted refutations, and will not get beyond the assertion that *different theories have different ranges of application.* But then it cannot possibly account for scientific progress. Instead of saying (as I should) that Newton's theory was falsified by crucial experiments which failed to falsify Einstein's, and that Einstein's theory is therefore better than Newton's, the consistent instrumentalist will have to say, with reference to his "new" point of view, like Heisenberg: "It follows that we do not say any longer: Newton's mechanics is false. . . . Rather, we now use the following formulation: Classical mechanics . . . is everywhere exactly 'right' where its concepts can be applied." [29]

[29] See W. Heisenberg in *Dialectica*, 2, 1948, p. 333 f. Heisenberg's own instrumentalism is far from consistent, and he has many anti-instrumentalist remarks to his credit. But this article here quoted may be described as an out-and-out attempt to prove that his quantum theory leads of necessity to an instrumentalist philosophy, and thereby to the result that physical theory can never be unified, or even made consistent.

Since "right" here means "applicable," this assertion merely amounts to saying, "Classical mechanics is applicable where its concepts can be applied"—which is not saying much. But be this as it may, the point is that *by neglecting falsification, and stressing application, instrumentalism proves to be as obscurantist a philosophy as essentialism.* For it is only in searching for refutations that science can hope to learn and to advance. It is only in considering how its various theories stand up to tests that it can distinguish between better and worse theories and so find a criterion of progress. (See chapter 10, of *Conjectures and Refutations.*)

Thus a mere instrument for prediction cannot be falsified. What may appear to us at first as its falsification turns out to be no more than a rider cautioning us about its limited applicability. This is why the instrumentalist view may be used *ad hoc* for rescuing a physical theory which is threatened by contradictions, as was done by Bohr (if I am right in my interpretation, given in section ii, of his principle of complementarity). If theories are mere instruments of prediction we need not discard any particular theory even though we believe that no consistent physical interpretation of its formalism exists.

Summing up we may say that instrumentalism is unable to account for the importance to pure science of testing severely even the most remote implications of its theories, since it is unable to account for the pure scientist's interest in truth and falsity. In contrast to the highly critical attitude requisite in the pure scientist, the attitude of instrumentalism (like that of applied science) is one of complacency at the success of applications. Thus it may well be responsible for the recent stagnation in quantum theory. (This was written before the refutation of parity.)

6. THE THIRD VIEW: CONJECTURES, TRUTH, AND REALITY

Neither Bacon nor Berkeley believed that the earth rotates, but nowadays everybody believes it, including the physicists. Instrumentalism is embraced by Bohr and Heisenberg only as a way out of the special difficulties which have arisen in quantum theory.

The motive is hardly sufficient. It is always difficult to interpret the latest theories, and they sometimes perplex even their own creators, as happened with Newton. Maxwell at first inclined to wards an essentialist interpretation of his theory: a theory which ultimately contributed more than any other to the decline of essentialism. And Einstein inclined at first to an instrumentalist interpretation of relativity, giving a kind of operational analysis of the concept of simultaneity which contributed more to the present vogue for instrumentalism than anything else; but he later repented.[30]

I trust that physicists will soon come to realize that the principle of complementarity is *ad hoc,* and (what is more important) that its only function is to avoid criticism and to prevent the discussion of physical interpretations; though criticism and discussion are urgently needed for reforming any theory. They will then no longer believe that instrumentalism is forced upon them by the structure of contemporary physical theory.

Anyway, instrumentalism is, as I have tried to show, no more acceptable than essentialism. Nor is there any need to accept either of them, for there is a third view.[31]

This "third view" is not very startling or even surprising, I think. It preserves the Galilean doctrine that the scientist aims at a true description of the world, or of some of its aspects, and at a true explanation of observable facts; and it combines this doctrine with the nonGalilean view that though this remains the aim of the scientist, he can never know for certain whether his findings are true, although he may sometimes establish with reasonable certainty that a theory is false.[32]

One may formulate this "third view" of scientific theories briefly by saying that they are *genuine conjectures*—highly informative guesses about the world which although not verifiable (*i.e.,* capable of being shown to be true) can be submitted to severe critical tests. They are serious attempts to discover the truth. In this respect scientific hypotheses are exactly like Goldbach's famous conjecture in the theory of numbers. Goldbach thought that it might possibly be true;

[30] *Note added to the proofs.* When this paper went to press Albert Einstein was still alive, and I intended to send him a copy as soon as it was printed. My remark referred to a conversation we had on the subject in 1950.

[31] Cf. section v of Chap. 6, of *Conjectures and Refutations.*

[32] Cf. the discussion of this point in section v, above, and *The Logic of Scientific Discovery (passim);* also Chap. 1 and Xenophanes' fragments quoted towards the end of Chap. 5, of *Conjectures and Refutations.*

and it may well be true in fact, even though *we do not know, and may perhaps never know, whether it is true or not.*

I shall confine myself to mentioning only a few aspects of my "third view," and only such aspects as distinguish it from essentialism and instrumentalism; and I shall take essentialism first.

Essentialism looks upon our ordinary world as mere appearance behind which it discovers the real world. This view has to be discarded once we become conscious of the fact that the world of each of our theories may be explained, in its turn, by further worlds which are described by further theories—theories of a higher level of abstraction, of universality, and of testability. The doctrine of an *essential or ultimate reality* collapses together with that of ultimate explanation.

Since according to our third view the new scientific theories are, like the old ones, genuine conjectures, they are genuine attempts to describe these further worlds. Thus we are led to take all these worlds, including our ordinary world, as equally real; or better, perhaps, as equally real aspects or layers of the real world. (If looking through a microscope we change its magnification, then we may see various completely different aspects or layers of the same thing, all equally real.) It is thus mistaken to say that my piano, as I know it, is real, while its alleged molecules and atoms are mere "logical constructions" (or whatever else may be indicative of their unreality); just as it is mistaken to say that atomic theory shows that the piano of my everyday world is an appearance only—a doctrine which is clearly unsatisfactory once we see that the atoms in their turn may perhaps be explained as disturbances, or structures of disturbances, in a quantised field of forces (or perhaps of probabilities). All these conjectures are equal in their claims to describe reality, although some of them are more conjectural than others.

Thus we shall not, for example, describe only the so-called "primary qualities" of a body (such as its geometrical shape) as real, and contrast them as the essentialists once did, with its unreal and merely apparent "secondary qualities" (such as colour). For the extension and even the shape of a body have since become *objects of explanation* in terms of theories of a higher level; of theories describing a further and deeper layer of reality—forces, and fields of forces—which are related to the primary qualities in the same way as these were believed by the essentialists to be related to the secondary ones; and the secondary qualities, such as colours, are just as real as the primary ones—though our colour experiences have to be distinguished from the colour-properties of the physical things, exactly as our geometrical-shape-experiences have to be distinguished from the geometrical-shape-properties of the physical things. From our point of view both kinds of qualities are equally real; and so are forces, and fields of forces—in spite of their undoubted hypothetical or conjectural character.

Although in one sense of the word "real," all these various levels are equally real, there is another yet closely related sense in which we might say that the higher and more conjectural levels are the *more real* ones—in spite of the fact that they are more conjectural. They are, according to our theories, more real (more stable in intention, more permanent) in the sense in which a table, or a tree, or a star, is more real than any of its aspects.

But is not just this conjectural or hypothetical character of our theories the reason why we should not ascribe reality to the worlds described by them? Should we not (even if we find Berkeley's "to be is to be perceived" too narrow) *call only those states of affairs "real" which are described by true statements,* rather than by conjectures which may turn out to be false? With these questions we turn to the discussion of the instrumentalist doctrine, which with its assertion that theories are mere instruments intends to deny the claim that anything like a real world is described by them.

I accept the view (implicit in the classical or correspondence theory of truth[33]) that we should call a state of affairs "real" if, and

[33] See A. Tarski's work on the *Concept of Truth* (*Der Wahrheitsbegriff, etc., Studia Philosophica,* 1935, text to note 1: "true = in agreement with reality"). (See the English translation in A. Tarski, *Logic, Semantics, Metamathematics,* 1956, p. 153; the translation says "corresponding" where I translated "in agreement.") The following remarks (and also the penultimate paragraph before the one to which this footnote is appended) have been added in an attempt to answer a friendly criticism privately communicated to me by Professor Alexander Koyré to whom I feel greatly indebted.

I do not think that, if we accept the suggestion that "in agreement with reality" and "true" are equivalent, we are seriously in danger of being led up the path to idealism. I do not propose to *define* "real" with the help of this equivalence. (And even if I did, there is no reason to believe that a definition necessarily determines the ontological status of the term defined.) What the equiva-

only if, the statement describing it is true. But it would be a grave mistake to conclude from this that the uncertainty of a theory, that is, its hypothetical or conjectural character, diminishes in any way its implicit *claim* to describe something real. For every statement *s* is equivalent to a statement claiming that *s* is true. And as to *s* being a conjecture, we must remember that, first of all, a conjecture *may* be true, and thus describe a real state of affairs. Secondly, if it is false, then it contradicts some real state of affairs (described by its true negation). Moreover, if we test our conjecture, and succeed in falsifying it, we see very clearly that there was a reality—something with which it could clash.

Our falsifications thus indicate the points where we have touched reality, as it were. And our latest and best theory is always an attempt to incorporate all the falsifications ever found in the field, by explaining them in the simplest way; and this means (as I have tried to show in *The Logic of Scientific Discovery*, sections 31 to 46) in the most testable way.

Admittedly, if we do not know how to test a theory we may be doubtful whether there is anything at all of the kind (or level) described by it; and if we positively know that it cannot be tested, then our doubts will grow; we may suspect that it is a mere myth, or a fairy tale. *But if a theory is testable, then it implies that events of a certain kind cannot happen; and so it asserts something about reality.* (This is why we demand that the more conjectural a theory is, the higher should be its degree of testability.) Testable conjectures or guesses, at any rate, are thus conjectures or guesses about reality; from their uncertain or conjectural character it only follows that our knowledge concerning the reality they describe is uncertain or conjectural. And although only that is certainly real which can be known with certainty, it is a mistake to think that only that is real which is known to be certainly real. We are not omniscient and, no doubt, much is real that is unknown to us all. It is thus indeed the old Berkeleian mistake (in the form "to be is to be known") which still underlies instrumentalism.

---

lence should help us to see is that the *hypothetical character* of a statement, *i.e.,* our *uncertainty as to its truth*—implies that we are making *guesses concerning reality.*

Theories are our own inventions, our own ideas; they are not forced upon us, but are our self-made instruments of thought: this has been clearly seen by the idealist. But some of these theories of ours can clash with reality; and when they do, we know that there is a reality; that there is something to remind us of the fact that our ideas may be mistaken. And this is why the realist is right.

Thus I agree with essentialism in its view that *science is capable of real discoveries,* and even in its view that in discovering new worlds our intellect triumphs over our sense experience. But I do not fall into the mistake of Parmenides—of denying reality to all that is colourful, varied, individual, indeterminate, and indescribable in our world.

Since I believe that science can make real discoveries I take my stand with Galileo against instrumentalism. I admit that our discoveries are conjectural. But this is even true of geographical explorations. Columbus' conjectures as to what he had discovered were in fact mistaken; and Peary could only conjecture—on the basis of theories—that he had reached the Pole. But these elements of conjecture do not make their discoveries less real, or less significant.

There is an important distinction which we can make between two kinds of scientific prediction, and which instrumentalism cannot make; a distinction which is connected with the problem of scientific discovery. I have in mind the distinction between the prediction of *events of a kind which is known,* such as eclipses or thunderstorms on the one hand and, on the other hand, the prediction of *new kinds of events* (which the physicist calls "new effects") such as the prediction which led to the discovery of wireless waves, or of zero-point energy, or to the artificial building up of new elements not previously found in nature.

It seems to me clear that instrumentalism can account only for the first kind of prediction: if theories are instruments for prediction, then we must assume that their purpose must be determined in advance, as with other instruments. Predictions of the second kind can be fully understood only as discoveries.

It is my belief that our discoveries are guided by theory in these as in most other cases, rather than that theories are the result of discoveries "due to observation"; for observation itself tends to be guided by theory. Even geographical discoveries (Columbus, Franklin, the two Nordenskjölds, Nansen, Wegener, and Heyerdahl's Kon-Tiki expedition) are often undertaken with the aim of testing a theory. Not to be content with offering predictions, but to create new situations for new kinds of tests: this is a function of theories which instrumentalism can hardly explain without surrendering its main tenets.

But perhaps the most interesting contrast between the "third view" and instrumentalism arises in connection with the latter's denial of the descriptive function of abstract words, and of disposition words. This doctrine, by the way, exhibits an essentialist strain within instrumentalism—the belief that events or occurrences or "incidents" (which are directly observable) must be, in a sense, more real than dispositions (which are not).

The "third view" of this matter is different. I hold that most observations are more or less indirect, and that it is doubtful whether the distinction between directly observable incidents and whatever is only indirectly observable leads us anywhere. I cannot but think that it is a mistake to denounce Newtonian forces (the "causes of acceleration") as occult, and to try to discard them (as has been suggested) in favour of accelerations. For accelerations cannot be observed any more directly than forces; and they are *just as dispositional:* the statement that a body's velocity is accelerated tells us that the body's velocity in the next second from now will exceed its present velocity.

In my opinion *all universals are dispositional.* If "breakable" is dispositional, so is "broken," considering for example how a doctor decides whether a bone is broken or not. Nor should we call a glass "broken" if the pieces would fuse the moment they were put together: the criterion of being broken is behaviour *under certain conditions.* Similarly, "red" is dispositional: a thing is red if it is able to reflect a certain kind of light—if it "looks red" in certain situations. But even "looking red" is dispositional. It describes the disposition of a thing to make onlookers agree that it looks red.

No doubt there are *degrees* of dispositional character: "able to conduct electricity" is dispositional in a higher degree than "conducting electricity now" which is still very highly dispositional. These degrees correspond fairly closely to those of the conjectural or hypothetical character of theories. But there is no point in denying reality to dispositions, not even if we deny reality to all universals and to all states of affairs, including incidents, and confine ourselves to using that sense of the word "real" which, from the point of view of ordinary usage, is the narrowest and safest: to call only physical bodies "real," and only those which are neither too small nor too big nor too distant to be easily seen and handled.

For even then we should realize (as I wrote twenty years ago[34]) that

> every description uses . . . universals; every statement has the character of a theory, a hypothesis. The statement, "Here is a glass of water," cannot be (completely) verified by any sense-experience, because the universals which appear in it cannot be correlated with any particular sense-experience. (An "immediate experience" is *only once* "immediately given"; it is unique.) By the word "glass," for example, we denote physical bodies which exhibit a certain *law-like behaviour;* and the same holds of the word "water."

I do not think that a language without universals could ever work; and the use of universals commits us to asserting, and thus (at least) to conjecturing, the reality of dispositions—though not of ultimate and inexplicable ones, that is, of essences. We may express all this by saying that the customary distinction between *"observational terms"* (or *"nontheoretical terms"*) and *theoretical terms* is mistaken, since all terms are theoretical to some degree, though some are more theortical than others; just as we said that all theories are conjectural, though some are more conjectural than others.

But if we are committed, or at least prepared, to conjecture the reality of forces, and of fields of forces, then there is no reason why we should not conjecture that a die has a definite *propensity* (or disposition) to fall on one or another of its sides; that this propensity can be changed by loading it; that propensities of this kind may change continuously; and that we may operate with fields of propensities, or of entities which determine propensities. An interpretation of probability on these lines might allow us to give a new physical interpretation to quantum theory—one which differs from the purely statistical interpretation, due to Born, while agreeing

[34] See *The Logic of Scientific Discovery,* end of section 25; see also new App. *x, (1) to (4); and Chap. 1 and Chap. 11, section v, text to notes 58–62 of *Conjectures and Refutations.*

with him that probability statements can be tested only statisically.[35]
And this interpretation may, perhaps, be of some little help in our
efforts to resolve those grave and challenging difficulties in quantum
theory which today seem to imperil the Galilean tradition.

[35] Concerning the propensity theory of probability, see my papers in *Observation and Interpretation*, ed. S. Körner 1957, pp. 65 ff., and in the *B.J.P.S.* 10, 1959,
pp. 25 ff.

J. L. AUSTIN

Other Minds

I feel that I agree with much, and especially with the more important
parts, of what Mr. Wisdom has written, both in his present paper
and in his beneficial series of articles on "Other Minds" and other
matters. I feel ruefully sure, also, that one must be at least one sort
of fool to rush in over ground so well trodden by the angels. At
best I can hope only to make a contribution to one part of the
problem, where it seems that a little more industry still might be
of service. I could only wish it was a more central part. In fact,
however, I did find myself unable to approach the centre while
still bogged down on the periphery. And Mr. Wisdom himself may
perhaps be sympathetic towards a policy of splitting hairs to save
starting them.

Mr. Wisdom, no doubt correctly, takes the "Predicament" to be
brought on by such questions as 'How do we know that another
man is angry?' He also cites other forms of the question—'Do we
(ever) know?," "Can we know?," "How can we know?" the thoughts,
feelings, sensations, mind, and so forth, of another creature, and
so forth. But it seems likely that each of these further questions is
rather different from the first, which alone has been enough to keep
me preoccupied, and to which I shall stick.

["Other Minds" was written as the second part of a symposium, the first part
of which was written by John Wisdom whose series of articles originally appeared in *Mind* and were published separately as *Other Minds*, 1952.—Editor]

* Reprinted from *Proceedings of the Aristotelian Society*, Supp. Vol. xx, 1946,
by courtesy of the Editor of the Aristotelian Society; copyright 1946, The Aristotelian Society.

Mr. Wisdom's method is to go on to ask: *Is it like the way in which we know* that a kettle is boiling, or that there is a tea party next door, or the weight of thistledown? But it seemed to me that perhaps, as he went on, he was not giving an altogether accurate account (perhaps only because too cursory a one) of what we should say if asked "How do you know?" these things. For example, in the case of the tea party, to say we knew of it "by analogy" would at best be a very sophisticated answer (and one to which some sophisticates might prefer the phrase "by induction"), while in addition it seems incorrect because we don't, I think, claim to *know* by analogy, but only to *argue* by analogy. Hence I was led on to consider what sort of thing does actually happen when ordinary people are asked "How do you know?"

Much depends, obviously, on the sort of item it is about which we are being asked "How do you know?" and there are bound to be many kinds of case that I shall not cover at all, or not in detail. The sort of statement which seems simplest, and at the same time not, on the face of it, unlike "He is angry," is such a statement as "That is a goldfinch" ("The kettle is boiling")—a statement of particular, current, empirical fact. This is the sort of statement on making which we are liable to be asked "How do you know?" and the sort that, at least sometimes, we say we don't know, but only believe. It may serve for a stalking-horse as well as another.

When we make an assertion such as "There is a goldfinch in the garden" or "He is angry," there is a sense in which we imply that we are sure of it or know it ("But I took it you *knew*," said reproachfully), though what we imply, in a similar sense and more strictly, is only that we *believe* it. On making such an assertion, therefore, we are directly exposed to the questions (1) "Do you *know* there is?" "Do you *know* he is?" and (2) "*How* do you know?" If in answer to the first question we reply "Yes," we may then be asked the second question, and even the first question alone is commonly taken as an invitation to state not merely *whether* but also *how* we know. But on the other hand, we may well reply "No" in answer to the first question: we may say "No, but I think there is," "No, but I believe he is." For the implication that I know or am sure is not strict: we are not all (terribly or sufficiently) strictly brought up. If we do this, then we are exposed to the question, which might also have been put to us without preliminaries, "Why do you believe that?" (or "What makes you think so?," "What induces you to suppose so?," &c.).

There is a singular difference between the two forms of challenge: "*How* do you know?" and "*Why* do you believe?" We seem never to ask "*Why* do you know?" or "*How* do you believe?" And in this, as well as in other respects to be noticed later, not merely such other words as "suppose," "assume," and so forth, but also the expressions "be sure" and "be certain," follow the example of "believe," not that of "know."

Either question, "How do you know?" or "Why do you believe?," may well be asked only out of respectful curiosity, from a genuine desire to learn. But again, they may both be asked as *pointed* questions, and, when they are so, a further difference comes out. "How do you know?" suggests that perhaps you *don't* know it at all, whereas "Why do you believe?" suggests that perhaps you *oughtn't* to believe it. There is no suggestion[1] that you *ought* not to know or that you *don't* believe it. If the answer to "How do you know?" or to "Why do you believe?" is considered unsatisfactory by the challenger, he proceeds rather differently in the two cases. His next riposte will be, on the one hand, something such as "Then you *don't* know any such thing," or "But that doesn't prove it: in that case you don't really know it at all," and on the other hand, something such as "That's very poor evidence to go on: you oughtn't to believe it on the strength of that alone." [2]

The "existence" of your alleged belief is not challenged, but the "existence" of your alleged knowledge *is* challenged. If we like to say that "I believe," and likewise "I am sure" and "I am certain," are descriptions of subjective mental or cognitive states or attitudes, or what not, then "I know" is not that, or at least not merely that: it functions differently in talking.

"But of course," it will be said, " 'I know' is obviously more than that, more than a description of my own state. If I *know, I can't be wrong.* You can always show I don't know by showing I am wrong, or may be wrong, or that I didn't know by showing that I might

---

[1] But in special senses and cases, there is, for example, if someone has announced some top secret information, we can ask, "How do *you* know?," nastily.

[2] An interesting variant in the case of knowing would be "You *oughtn't to say* (you've no business to say) you know it at all." But of course this is only superficially similar to "You oughtn't to believe it": you ought *to say* you believe it, if you do believe it, however poor the evidence.

have been wrong. *That's* the way in which knowing differs even from being as certain as can be." This must be considered in due course, but first we should consider the types of answer that may be given in answer to the question "How do you know?"

Suppose I have said "There's a bittern at the bottom of the garden," and you ask "How do you know?" my reply may take very different forms:

(a) I was brought up in the fens
(b) I heard it
(c) The keeper reported it
(d) By its booming
(e) From the booming noise
(f) Because it is booming.

We may say, roughly, that the first three are answers to the questions "How do you come to know?," "How are you in a position to know?," or "How do *you* know?" understood in different ways: while the other three are answers to "How can you tell?" understood in different ways. That is, I may take you to have been asking:

(1) How do I come to be in a position to know about bitterns?
(2) How do I come to be in a position to say there's a bittern here and now?
(3) How do (can) I tell bitterns?
(4) How do (can) I tell the thing here and now as a bittern?

The implication is that in order to know this is a bittern, I must have:

(1) been trained in an environment where I could become familiar with bitterns
(2) had a certain opportunity in the current case
(3) learned to recognize or tell bitterns
(4) succeeded in recognizing or telling this as a bittern.

(1) and (2) mean that my experiences must have been of certain kinds, that I must have had certain opportunities: (3) and (4) mean that I must have exerted a certain kind and amount of acumen.[3]

---

[3] "I know, I *know*, I've seen it a hundred times, don't keep on telling me" complains of a superabundance of opportunity: "knowing a hawk from a hand-saw" lays down a minimum of acumen in recognition or classification. "As well as I know my own name" is said to typify something I *must* have experienced and *must* have learned to discriminate.

The questions raised in (1) and (3) concern our *past* experiences, our opportunities and our activities in learning to discriminate or discern, and, bound up with both, the correctness or otherwise of the linguistic usages we have acquired. Upon these earlier experiences depends how *well* we know things, just as, in different but cognate cases of "knowing," it is upon earlier experience that it depends how *thoroughly* or how *intimately* we know: we know a person by sight or intimately, a town inside out, a proof backwards, a job in every detail, a poem word for word, a Frenchman when we see one. "He doesn't know what love (real hunger) is" means he hasn't had enough experience to be able to recognize it and to distinguish it from other things slightly like it. According to how well I know an item, and according to the kind of item it is, I can recognize it, describe it, reproduce it, draw it, recite it, apply it, and so forth. Statements like "I know *very well* he isn't angry" or "You know *very well* that isn't calico," though of course about the current case, ascribe the excellence of the knowledge to past experience, as does the general expression "You are old enough to know better." [4]

By contrast, the questions raised in (2) and (4) concern the circumstances of the current case. Here we can ask "How *definitely* do you know?" You may know it for certain, quite positively, officially, on his own authority, from unimpeachable sources, only indirectly, and so forth.

Some of the answers to the question "How do you know?" are, oddly enough, described as "reasons for knowing" or "reasons to know," or even sometimes as "reasons why I know," despite the fact that we do not ask "Why do you know?" But now surely, according to the Dictionary, "reasons" should be given in answer to the question "Why?" just as we do in fact give reasons for believing in answer to the question "Why do you believe?" However there is a distinction to be drawn here. "How do you know that I. G. Farben worked for war?" "I have every reason to know: I served on the investigating commission": here, giving my reasons for knowing is stating how I come to be in a position to know. In the same way we use the expression "I know *because* I saw him do it" or "I know

---

[4] The adverbs that can be inserted in "How . . . do you know?" are few in number and fall into still fewer classes. There is practically no overlap with those that can be inserted in "How . . . do you believe?" (firmly, sincerely, genuinely, &c.).

because I looked it up only ten minutes ago": these are similar to "So it is: it *is* plutonium. How did you know?" "I did quite a bit of physics at school before I took up philology," or to "I ought to know: I was standing only a couple of yards away." Reasons for *believing* on the other hand are normally quite a different affair (a recital of symptoms, arguments in support, and so forth), though there are cases where we do give as reasons for believing our having been in a position in which we could get good evidence: "Why do you believe he was lying?" "I was watching him very closely."

Among the cases where we give our reasons for knowing things, a special and important class is formed by those where we cite authorities. If asked "How do you know the election is today?," I am apt to reply "I read it in *The Times*," and if asked "How do you know the Persians were defeated at Marathon?" I am apt to reply "Herodotus expressly states that they were." In these cases "know" is correctly used: we know "at second hand" when we can cite an authority who was in a position to know (possibly himself also only at second hand).[5] The statement of an authority makes me aware of something, enables me to know something, which I shouldn't otherwise have known. It is a source of knowledge. In many cases, we contrast such reasons for knowing with other reasons for believing the very same thing: "Even if we didn't know it, even if he hadn't confessed, the evidence against him would be enough to hang him."

It is evident, of course, that this sort of "knowledge" is "liable to be wrong," owing to the unreliability of human testimony (bias, mistake, lying, exaggeration, &c.). Nevertheless, the occurrence of a piece of human testimony radically alters the situation. We say "We shall never know what Caesar's feelings were on the field of the battle of Philippi," because he did not pen an account of them: *if* he *had*, then to say "We shall never know" won't do in the same way, even though we may still perhaps find reason to say "It doesn't

---

[5] Knowing at second hand, or on authority, is not the same as "knowing indirectly," whatever precisely that difficult and perhaps artificial expression may mean. If a murderer "confesses," then, whatever our opinion of the worth of the "confession," we cannot say that "we (only) know indirectly that he did it," nor can we so speak when a witness, reliable or unreliable, has stated that he saw the man do it. Consequently, it is not correct, either, to say that the murderer himself knows "directly" that he did it, whatever precisely "knowing directly" may mean.

read very plausibly: we shall never *really* know the *truth*" and so on. Naturally, we are judicious: we don't say we know (at second hand) if there is any special reason to doubt the testimony: but there has to be *some* reason. It is fundamental in talking (as in other matters) that we are entitled to trust others, except in so far as there is some concrete reason to distrust them. Believing persons, accepting testimony, is the, or one main, point of talking. We don't play (competitive) games except in the faith that our opponent is trying to win: if he isn't, it isn't a game, but something different. So we don't talk with people (descriptively) except in the faith that they are trying to convey information.[6]

It is now time to turn to the question "How can you tell?," that is, to senses (2) and (4) of the question "How do you know?" If you have asked "How do you know it's a goldfinch?" then I may reply "From its behaviour," "By its markings," or, in more detail, "By its red head," "From its eating thistles." That is, I indicate, or to some extent set out with some degree of precision, those features of the situation which enable me to recognize it as one to be described in the way I did describe it. Thereupon you may still object in several ways to my saying it's a goldfinch, without in the least "disputing my facts," which is a further stage to be dealt with later. You may object:

(1) But goldfinches *don't* have red heads
(1a) But that's not a *goldfinch*. From your own description I can recognize it as a gold*crest*
(2) But that's not enough: plenty of other birds have red heads. What you say doesn't prove it. For all you know, it may be a woodpecker.

Objections (1) and (1a) claim that, in one way or another, I am evidently unable to recognize goldfinches. It may be (1a)—that I have not learned the right (customary, popular, official) name to apply to the creature ("Who taught you to use the word 'goldfinch'?"):[7] or it may be that my powers of discernment, and con-

---

[6] Reliance on the authority of others is fundamental, too, in various special matters, for example, for corroboration and for the correctness of our own use of words, which we learn from others.

[7] Misnaming is not a trivial or laughing matter. If I misname I shall mislead others, and I shall also misunderstand information given by others to me. "Of course I knew all about his condition perfectly, but I never realized that was

sequently of classification, have never been brought sharply to bear in these matters, so that I remain confused as to how to tell the various species of small British bird. Or, of course, it may be a bit of both. In making this sort of accusation, you would perhaps tend not so much to use the expression "You don't know" or "You oughtn't to say you know" as, rather, "But that *isn't* a goldfinch (*goldfinch*)," or "Then you're wrong to call it a goldfinch." But still, if asked, you would of course deny the statement that I do know it is a goldfinch.

It is in the case of objection (2) that you would be more inclined to say right out "Then you don't know." Because it doesn't prove it, it's not enough to prove it. Several important points come out here:

(*a*) If you say "That's not enough," then you must have in mind some more or less definite lack. "To be a goldfinch, besides having a red head it must also have the characteristic eye-markings": or "How do you know it isn't a woodpecker? Woodpeckers have red heads too." If there is no definite lack, which you are at least prepared to specify on being pressed, then it's silly (outrageous) just to go on saying "That's not enough."

(*b*) Enough is enough: it doesn't mean everything. Enough means enough to show that (within reason, and for present intents and purposes) it "can't" be anything else, there is no room for an alternative, competing, description of it. It does *not* mean, for example, enough to show it isn't a *stuffed* goldfinch.

(*c*) "*From* its red head," given as an answer to "How do you know?" requires careful consideration: in particular it differs very materially from "*Because* it has a red head," which is also sometimes given as an answer to "How do you know?," and is commonly given as an answer to "Why do you believe?" It is much more akin to such obviously "vague" replies as "From its markings" or "From its behaviour" than at first appears. Our claim, in saying we know (*i.e.*, that we can tell) is to *recognize*: and recognizing, at least in this sort of case, consists in seeing, or otherwise sensing, a feature or features which we are sure are similar to something noted (and

---

diabetes: I thought it was cancer, and all the books agree that's incurable: if I'd only known it was diabetes, I should have thought of insulin at once." Knowing *what a thing is* is, to an important extent, knowing what the name for it, and the right name for it, is.

usually named) before, on some earlier occasion in our experience. But, this that we see, or otherwise sense, is not necessarily *describable in words*, still less describable in detail, and in noncommittal words, and by anybody you please. Nearly everybody can recognize a surly look or the smell of tar, but few can describe them noncommittally, that is, otherwise than as "surly" or "of tar": many can recognize, and "with certainty," ports of different vintages, models by different fashion houses, shades of green, motorcar makes from behind, and so forth, without being able to say "*how* they recognize them," that is, without being able to "be more specific about it"—they can only say they can tell "by the taste," "from the cut," and so on. So, when I say I can tell the bird "from its red head," or that I know a friend "by his nose," I imply that there is something *peculiar* about the red head or the nose, something peculiar to goldfinches or to him, by which you can (always) tell them or him. In view of the fewness and crudeness of the classificatory words in any language compared with the infinite number of features which are recognized, or which could be picked out and recognized, in our experience, it is small wonder that we often and often fall back on the phrases beginning with "from" and "by," and that we are not able to *say*, further and precisely, *how* we can tell. Often we know things quite well, while scarcely able at all to say "from" what we know them, let alone what there is so very special about them. Any answer beginning "From" or "By" has, intentionally, this saving "vagueness." But on the contrary, an answer beginning "Because" is dangerously definite. When I say I know it's a goldfinch "Because it has a red head," that implies that all I have noted, or needed to note, about it is that its head is red (nothing special or peculiar about the shade, shape, and so forth of the patch): so that I imply that there is no other small British bird that has any sort of red head except the goldfinch.

(*d*) Whenever I say I know, I am always liable to be taken to claim that, in a certain sense appropriate to the kind of statement (and to present intents and purposes), I am able to *prove* it. In the present, very common, type of case, "proving" seems to mean stating what are the features of the current case which are enough to constitute it one which is correctly describable in the way we have described it, and not in any other way relevantly variant. Generally speaking, cases where I can "prove" are cases where we use the "because" formula: cases where we "know but can't prove" are cases where we take refuge in the "from" or "by" formula.

I believe that the points so far raised are those most genuinely and normally raised by the question "How do you know?" But there are other, further, questions sometimes raised under the same rubric, and especially by philosophers, which may be thought more important. These are the worries about "reality" and about being "sure and certain."

Up to now, in challenging me with the question "How do you know?," you are not taken to have *queried my credentials as stated,* though you have asked what they were: nor have you *disputed my facts* (the facts on which I am relying to prove it is a goldfinch), though you have asked me to detail them. It is this further sort of challenge that may now be made, a challenge as to the *reliability* of our alleged "credentials" and our alleged "facts." You may ask:

(1) But do you know it's a *real* goldfinch? How do you know you're not dreaming? Or after all, mightn't it be a stuffed one? And is the head really red? Couldn't it have been dyed, or isn't there perhaps an odd light reflected on it?

(2) But are you certain it's the *right* red for a goldfinch? Are you quite sure it isn't too orange? Isn't it perhaps rather too strident a note for a bittern?

These two sorts of worry are distinct, though very probably they can be combined or confused, or may run into one another: for example, "Are you sure it's really red?" may mean "Are you sure it isn't orange?" or again "Are you sure it isn't just the peculiar light?"

1. REALITY

If you ask me, "How do you know it's a real stick?" "How do you know it's really bent?" ("Are you sure he's really angry?"), then you are querying my credentials or my facts (it's often uncertain which) in a certain special way. In various *special, recognized* ways, depending essentially upon the nature of the matter which I have announced myself to know, either my current experiencing or the item currently under consideration (or uncertain which) may be abnormal, *phoney.* Either I myself may be dreaming, or in delirium, or under the influence of mescal, and so forth: or else the item may be stuffed, painted, dummy, artificial, trick, freak, toy, assumed, feigned, and so forth: or else again there's an uncertainty (it's left open) whether *I* am to blame or *it* is—mirages, mirror images, odd lighting effects, and so forth.

These doubts are all to be allayed by means of recognized procedures (more or less roughly recognized, of course), appropriate to the particular type of case. There are recognized ways of distinguishing between dreaming and waking (how otherwise should we know how to use and to contrast the words?), and of deciding whether a thing is stuffed or live, and so forth. The doubt or question "But is it a *real* one?" has always (*must* have) a special basis, there must be some "reason for suggesting" that it isn't real, in the sense of some specific way, or limited number of specific ways, in which it is suggested that this experience or item may be phoney. Sometimes (usually) the context makes it clear what the suggestion is: the goldfinch might be stuffed but there's no suggestion that it's a mirage, the oasis might be a mirage but there's no suggestion it might be stuffed. If the context doesn't make it clear, then I am entitled to ask "How do you mean? Do you mean it may be stuffed or what? *What are you suggesting*?" The wile of the metaphysician consists in asking "Is it a real table?" (a kind of object which has no obvious way of being phoney) and not specifying or limiting what may be wrong with it, so that I feel at a loss "how to prove" it *is* a real one.[8] It is the use of the word "real" in this manner that leads us on to the supposition that "real" has a single meaning ("the real world" "material objects"), and that a highly profound and puzzling one. Instead, we should insist always on specifying with what "real" is being contrasted—"not what" I shall have to show it is, in order to show it is "real": and then usually we shall find some specific, less fatal, word, appropriate to the particular case, to substitute for "real."

Knowing it's a "real" goldfinch isn't in question in the ordinary case when I say I know it's a goldfinch: reasonable precautions only are taken. But when it *is* called in question, in *special* cases, then I make sure it's a real goldfinch in ways essentially similar to those

---

[8] Conjurers, too, trade on this. "Will some gentleman kindly satisfy himself that this is a perfectly ordinary hat?" This leaves us baffled and uneasy: sheepishly we agree that it seems all right, while conscious that we have not the least idea what to guard against.

in which I made sure it was a goldfinch, though corroboration by other witnesses plays a specially important part in some cases. Once again the precautions cannot be more than reasonable, relative to current intents and purposes. And once again, in the special cases just as in the ordinary cases, two further conditions hold good:

(a) I don't by any means *always* know whether it's one or not. It may fly away before I have a chance of testing it, or of inspecting it thoroughly enough. This is simple enough: yet some are prone to argue that because I *sometimes* don't know or can't discover, I *never* can.

(b) "Being sure it's real" is no more proof against miracles or outrages of nature than anything else is or, *sub specie humanitatis,* can be. If we have made sure it's a goldfinch, and a real goldfinch, and then in the future it does something outrageous (explodes, quotes Mrs. Woolf, or what not), we don't say we were wrong to say it was a goldfinch, *we don't know what to say.* Words literally fail us: "What would you have said?" "What are we to say now?" "What would *you* say?" When I have made sure it's a real goldfinch (not stuffed, corroborated by the disinterested, &c.) then I am *not* "predicting" in saying it's a real goldfinch, and in a very good sense I can't be proved wrong whatever happens. It seems a serious mistake to suppose that language (or most language, language about real things) is "predictive" in such a way that the future can always prove it wrong. What the future *can* always do, is to make us *revise our ideas* about goldfinches or real goldfinches or anything else.

Perhaps the normal procedure of language could be schematized as follows. First, it is arranged that, on experiencing a complex of features C, then we are to say "This is C" or "This is a C." Then subsequently, the occurrence either of the whole of C or of a significant and characteristic part of it is, on one or many occasions, accompanied or followed in definite circumstances by another special and distinctive feature or complex of features, which makes it seem desirable to revise our ideas: so that we draw a distinction between "This looks like a C, but in fact is only a dummy, and so forth" and "This is a real C (live, genuine, &c.)." *Henceforward,* we can only ascertain that it's a *real* C by ascertaining that the special feature or complex of features is present in the appropriate circumstances. The old expression "This is a C" will tend as heretofore to fail to draw any distinction between "real, live, and so forth" and "dummy, stuffed, &c." If the special distinctive feature is one which does not have to manifest itself in *any* definite circumstances (on application of some specific test, after some limited lapse of time, &c.) then it is not a suitable feature on which to base a distinction between "real" and "dummy, imaginary, and so forth." All we can then do is to say "Some Cs are and some aren't, some do and some don't: and it may be very interesting or important whether they are or aren't, whether they do or don't, but they're all Cs, real Cs, just the same." [9] Now if the special feature is one which must appear in (more or less) definite circumstances, then "This is a real C" is not necessarily predictive: we can, in favourable cases, make sure of it.[10]

2. SURENESS AND CERTAINTY

The other way of querying my credentials and proofs ("Are you sure it's the *right* red?") is quite different. Here we come up against Mr. Wisdom's views on "the peculiarity of a man's knowledge of his own sensations," for which he refers us to "Other Minds VII" (*Mind*, Vol. lii, N.S., No. 207), a passage with which I find I disagree.

Mr. Wisdom there says that, excluding from consideration cases like "being in love" and other cases which "involve prediction," and considering statements like "I am in pain" which, in the requisite sense, do *not* involve prediction, then a man *cannot* "be wrong" in making them, in the most favoured sense of being wrong: that is, though it is of course possible for him to *lie* (so that "I am in pain" may be false), and though it is also possible for him to *misname*, that is, to use the word "pawn," say, instead of "pain," which would be liable to mislead others but would not mislead himself, either because he regularly uses "pawn" for "pain" or because the use was a momentary aberration, as when I call John "Albert" while knowing him quite well to be John—though it is possible for him to be "wrong" in these two senses, it is not possible for him to be wrong

[9] The awkwardness about some snarks being boojums.
[10] Sometimes, on the basis of the new special feature, we distinguish, not between "Cs" and "real Cs," but rather between Cs and Ds. There is a reason for choosing the one procedure rather than the other: all cases where we use the "real" formula exhibit (complicated and serpentine) likenesses, as do all cases where we use "proper," a word which behaves in many ways like "real," and is no less nor more profound.

in the most favoured sense. He says again that, with this class of statement (elsewhere called "sense statements"), to know directly that one is in pain is "to say that one is, and to say it on the basis of being in pain": and again, that the peculiarity of sense statements lies in the fact that "when they are correct and made by X, then X knows they are correct."

This seems to me mistaken, though it is a view that, in more or less subtle forms, has been the basis of a very great deal of philosophy. It is perhaps the original sin (Berkeley's apple, the tree in the quad) by which the philosopher casts himself out from the garden of the world we live in.

Very clearly detailed, this is the view that, at least and only in a certain favoured type of case, I can "say what I see (or otherwise sense)" almost quite literally. On this view, if I were to say "Here is something red," then I might be held to imply or to state that it is really a red thing, a thing which would appear red in a standard light, or to other people, or tomorrow too, and perhaps even more besides: all of which "involves prediction" (if not also a metaphysical substratum). Even if I were to say "Here is something which looks red," I might still be held to imply or to state that it looks red to others also, and so forth. If, however, I confine myself to stating "Here is something that looks red to me now," then at last I can't be wrong (in the most favoured sense).

However, there is an ambiguity in "something that looks red to me now." Perhaps this can be brought out by italics, though it is not really so much a matter of emphasis as of tone and expression, of confidence and hesitancy. Contrast "Here is something that (definitely) *looks to me* (anyhow) red" with "Here is something that looks to me (something like) *red* (I should say)." In the former case I am quite confident that, however it may look to others, whatever it may "really be," and so forth, it certainly does look red to me at the moment. In the other case I'm not confident at all: it looks reddish, but I've never seen anything quite like it before, I can't quite describe it—or, I'm not very good at recognizing colours, I never feel quite happy about them, I've constantly been caught out about them. Of course, this sounds silly in the case of "red": red is so *very* obvious, we all know red when we see it, it's *unmistakable*.[11]

---

[11] And yet she always *thought* his shirt was white until she saw it against Tommy's Persil-washed one.

Cases where we should not feel happy about red are not easy (though not impossible) to find. But take "magenta": "It looks rather like magenta to me—but then I wouldn't be too sure about distinguishing magenta from mauve or from heliotrope. Of course I know in a way it's purplish, but I don't really know whether to say it's magenta or not: I just can't be sure." Here, I am not interested in ruling out consideration of how it looks to others (looks *to me*) or considerations about what its *real* colour is (*looks*): what I am ruling out is *my being sure or certain* what it looks to me. Take tastes, or take sounds: these are so much better as examples than colours, because we never feel so happy with our other senses as with our eyesight. Any description of a taste or sound or smell (or colour) or of a feeling, involves (is) saying that it is like one or some that we have experienced before: any descriptive word is classificatory, involves recognition and in that sense memory, and only when we use such words (or names or descriptions, which come down to the same) are we knowing anything, or believing anything. But memory and recognition are often uncertain and unreliable.

Two rather different ways of being hesitant may be distinguished.

(*a*) Let us take the case where we are tasting a certain taste. We may say "I simply don't know what it is: I've never tasted anything remotely like it before. . . . No, it's no use: the more I think about it the more confused I get: it's perfectly distinct and perfectly distinctive, quite unique in my experience." This illustrates the case where I can find nothing in my past experience with which to compare the current case: I'm certain it's not appreciably like anything I ever tasted before, not sufficiently like anything I know to merit the same description. This case, though distinguishable enough, shades off into the more common type of case where I'm not quite certain, or only fairly certain, or practically certain, that it's the taste of, say, laurel. In all such cases, I am endeavouring to recognize the current item by searching in my past experience for something like it, some likeness in virtue of which it deserves, more or less positively, to be described by the same descriptive word:[12] and I am meeting with varying degrees of success.

(*b*) The other case is different, though it very naturally combines

---

[12] Or, of course, related to it in some other way than by "similarity" (in any ordinary sense of "similarity"), which is yet sufficient reason for describing it by the same word.

itself with the first. Here, what I try to do is to *savour* the current experience, to *peer* at it, to sense it vividly. I'm not sure it *is* the taste of pineapple: isn't there perhaps just *something* about it, a *tang*, a bite, a lack of bite, a cloying sensation, which isn't *quite* right for pineapple? Isn't there perhaps just a peculiar hint of green, which would rule out mauve and would hardly do for heliotrope? Or perhaps it is faintly odd: I must look more intently, scan it over and over: maybe just possibly there is a suggestion of an unnatural shimmer, so that it doesn't look quite like ordinary water. There is a lack of sharpness in what we actually sense, which is to be cured not, or not merely, by thinking, but by acuter discernment, by sensory discrimination (though it is of course true that thinking of other, and more pronounced, cases in our past experience can and does assist our powers of discrimination).[13]

Cases (*a*) and (*b*) alike, and perhaps usually together, lead to our being not quite sure or certain what it is, what to say, how to describe it: what our feelings really are, whether the tickling is painful exactly, whether I'm really what you'd call angry with him or only something rather like it. The hesitation is of course, in a sense, over misnaming: but I am not so much or merely worried about possibly misleading others as about misleading myself (the most favoured sense of being wrong). I should suggest that the two expressions "being certain" and "being sure," though from the nature of the case they are often used indiscriminately, have a tendency to refer to cases (*a*) and (*b*) respectively. "Being certain" tends to indicate confidence in our memories and our past discernment, "being sure" to indicate confidence in the current perception. Perhaps this comes out in our use of the concessives "to be sure" and "certainly," and in our use of such phrases as "certainly not" and "surely not." But it may be unwise to chivvy language beyond the coarser nuances.

It may be said that, even when I don't know exactly how to describe it, I nevertheless *know* that I *think* (and roughly how confidently I think) it is mauve. So I do know *something*. But this is irrelevant: I *don't* know it's mauve, that it definitely looks to me now mauve. Besides, there are cases where I really don't know what I think: I'm completely baffled by it.

Of course, there are any number of "sense statements" about

[13] This appears to cover cases of dull or careless or uninstructed perception, as opposed to cases of diseased or drugged perception.

which I can be, and am, completely sure. In ordinary cases ordinary men are nearly always certain when a thing looks red (or reddish, or anyhow reddish rather than greenish), or when they're in pain (except when that's rather difficult to say, as when they're being tickled): in ordinary cases an expert, a dyer or a dress designer, will be quite sure when something looks (to him in the present light) reseda green or nigger brown, though those who are not experts will not be so sure. Nearly always, if not quite always, we can be quite, or pretty, sure if we take refuge in a sufficiently *rough* description of the sensation: roughness and sureness tend to vary inversely. But the less rough descriptions, just as much as the rough, are all "sense statements."

It is, I think, the problems of sureness and certainty, which philosophers tend (if I am not mistaken) to neglect, that have considerably exercised scientists, while the problem of "reality," which philosophers have cultivated, does not exercise them. The whole apparatus of measures and standards seems designed to combat unsureness and uncertainty, and concomitantly to increase the possible precision of language, which, in science, pays. But for the words "real" and "unreal" the scientist tends to substitute, wisely, their cash value substitutes, of which he invents and defines an increasing number, to cover an increasing variety of cases: he doesn't ask "Is it real?" but rather "Is it denatured?" or "Is it an allotropic form?" and so on.

It is not clear to me what the class of sense statements is, nor what its "peculiarity" is. Some who talk of sense statements (or sense data) appear to draw a distinction between talking about simple things like red or pain, and talking about complicated things like love or tables. But apparently Mr. Wisdom does not, because he treats "This looks to me now like a man eating poppies" as in the same case with "This looks to me now red." In this he is surely right: a man eating poppies may be more "complex" to recognize, but it is often not appreciably more difficult than the other. But if, again, we say that nonsense statements are those which involve "prediction," why so? True, if I say, "This is a (real) oasis" without first ascertaining that it's not a mirage, then I do chance my hand: but if I *have* ascertained that it's not, and can recognize for sure that it isn't (as when I am drinking its waters), then surely I'm not chancing my hand any longer. I believe, of course, that it will continue to perform as (real) oases normally do: but if there's a *lusus naturae,* a miracle, and it doesn't, that wouldn't mean I was wrong, previously, to call it a real oasis.

With regard to Mr. Wisdom's own chosen formulae, we have seen already that it can't be right to say that the peculiarity of sense statements is that "when they are correct, and made by X, then X knows they are correct": for X may *think,* without much confidence, that it tastes to him like Lapsang, and yet be far from certain, and then subsequently become certain, or more certain, that it did or didn't. The other two formulae were: "To know that one is in pain is to say that one is and to say it on the basis of being in pain" and that the only mistake possible with sense statements is typified by the case where "knowing him to be Jack I call him 'Alfred,' thinking his name is Alfred or not caring a damn what his name is." The snag in both these lies in the phrases "on the basis of being in pain" and "knowing him to be Jack." "Knowing him to be Jack" means that I have recognized him as Jack, a matter over which I may well be hesitant and/or mistaken: it is true that I needn't recognize him *by name* as "Jack" (and hence I may call him "Alfred"), but at least I must be recognizing him correctly as, for instance, the man I last saw in Jerusalem, or else I *shall* be misleading *myself.* Similarly, if "on the basis of being in pain" only means "when I am (what would be correctly described as) in pain," then something more than merely *saying* "I'm in pain" is necessary for knowing I'm in pain: and this something more, as it involves recognition, may be hesitant and/or mistaken, though it is of course unlikely to be so in a case so comparatively obvious as that of pain.

Possibly the tendency to overlook the problems of recognition is fostered by the tendency to use a direct object after the word *know.* Mr. Wisdom, for example, confidently uses such expressions as "knowing the feelings of another (his mind, his sensations, his anger, his pain) in the way that *he* knows them." But, although we do correctly use the expressions "I know your feelings on the matter" or "He knows his own mind" or (archaically) "May I know your mind?," these are rather special expressions, which do not justify any general usage. "Feelings" here has the sense it has in "very strong feelings" in favour of or against something: perhaps it means "views" or "opinions" ("very decided opinions"), just as "mind" in this usage is given by the Dictionary as equivalent to "intention" or "wish." To extend the usage uncritically is somewhat as though, on the strength of the legitimate phrase "knowing someone's tastes," we were to proceed to talk of "knowing someone's sounds" or "knowing someone's taste of pineapple." If, for example, it is a case of *physical* feelings such as fatigue, we do not use the expression "I know your feelings."

When, therefore, Mr. Wisdom speaks generally of "knowing his sensations," he presumably means this to be equivalent to "knowing *what* he is seeing, smelling, and so forth," just as "knowing the winner of the Derby" means "knowing *what won* the Derby." But here again, the expression "know what" seems sometimes to be taken, unconsciously and erroneously, to lend support to the practice of putting a direct object after *know:* for "what" is liable to be understood as a relative, = "that which." This is a grammatical mistake: "what" *can* of course be a relative, but in "know what you feel" and "know what won" it is an interrogative (Latin *quid,* not *quod*). In this respect, "I can smell what he is smelling" differs from "I can know what he is smelling." "I know what he is feeling" is not "There is an *x* which both I know and he is feeling," but "I know the answer to the question 'What is he feeling?'" And similarly with "I know what I am feeling": this does *not* mean that there is something which I am *both knowing and feeling*.

Expressions such as "We don't know another man's anger in the way he knows it" or "He knows his pain in a way we can't" seem barbarous. The man doesn't "know his pain": he feels (not knows) what he recognizes as, or what he knows to be, anger (not his anger), and he knows that he is feeling angry. Always assuming that he does recognize the feeling, which in fact, though feeling it acutely, he may not: "Now I know what it was, it was jealousy (or gooseflesh or angina). At the time I did not know at all what it was, I had never felt anything quite like it before: but since then I've got to know it quite well." [14]

Uncritical use of the direct object after *know* seems to be one thing that leads to the view that (or to talking as though) sensa,

---

[14] There are, of course, legitimate uses of the direct object after *know,* and of the possessive pronoun before words for feelings. "He knows the town well," "He has known much suffering," "My old vanity, how well I know it!"—even the pleonastic "Where does he feel his (= the) pain?" and the educative tautology "*He* feels *his* pain." But none of these really lends support to the metaphysical "He knows his pain (in a way we can't)."

that is things, colours, noises, and the rest, speak or are labelled by nature, so that I can literally *say* what (that which) I *see:* it pipes up, or I read it off. It is as if sensa were *literally* to "announce themselves" or to "identify themselves," in the way we indicate when we say "It presently identified itself as a particularly fine white rhinoceros." But surely this is only a manner of speaking, a reflexive idiom in which the French, for example, indulge more freely than the English: sensa are dumb, and only previous experience enables *us* to identify them. If we choose to say that they "identify themselves" (and certainly "recognizing" is not a highly voluntary activity of ours), then it must be admitted that they share the birthright of all speakers, that of speaking unclearly and untruly.

IF I KNOW I CAN'T BE WRONG

One final point about "How do you know?," the challenge to the user of the expression "I know," requires still to be brought out by consideration of the saying that "If you know you can't be wrong." Surely, if what has so far been said is correct, then we are often right to say we *know* even in cases where we turn out subsequently to have been mistaken—and indeed we seem always, or practically always, liable to be mistaken.

Now, we are perfectly, and should be candidly, aware of this liability, which does not, however, transpire to be so very onerous in practice. The human intellect and senses are, indeed, *inherently* fallible and delusive, but not by any means *inveterately* so. Machines are inherently liable to break down, but good machines don't (often). It is futile to embark on a "theory of knowledge" which denies this liability: such theories constantly end up by admitting the liability after all, and denying the existence of "knowledge."

"When you know you can't be wrong" is perfectly good sense. You are prohibited from saying "I know it is so, but I may be wrong," just as you are prohibited from saying "I promise I will, but I may fail." If you are aware you may be mistaken, you ought not to say you know, just as, if you are aware you may break your word, you have no business to promise. But of course, being aware that you may be mistaken doesn't mean merely being aware that you are a fallible human being: it means that you have some concrete reason to suppose that you may be mistaken in this case. Just as "but I may fail" does not mean merely "but I am a weak human being" (in which case it would be no more exciting than adding "D.V."): it means that there is some concrete reason for me to suppose that I shall break my word. It is naturally *always* possible ("humanly" possible) that I may be mistaken or may break my word, but that by itself is no bar against using the expressions "I know" and "I promise" as we do in fact use them.

At the risk (long since incurred) of being tedious, the parallel between saying "I know" and saying "I promise" may be elaborated.[15]

When I say "S is P," I imply at least that I believe it, and, if I have been strictly brought up, that I am (quite) sure of it: when I say "I shall do A," I imply at least that I hope to do it, and, if I have been strictly brought up that I (fully) intend to. If I only believe that S is P, I can add "But of course I may (very well) be wrong": if I only hope to do A, I can add "But of course I may (very well) not." When I only believe or only hope, it is recognized that further evidence or further circumstances are liable to make me change my mind. If I say "S is P" when I don't even believe it, I am lying: if I say it when I believe it but am not sure of it, I may be misleading but I am not exactly lying. If I say "I shall do A" when I have not even any hope, not the slightest intention, of doing it, then I am deliberately deceiving: if I say it when I do not fully intend to, I am misleading but I am not deliberately deceiving in the same way.

But now, when I say "I promise," a new plunge is taken: I have not merely announced my intention, but, by using this formula (performing this ritual), I have bound myself to others, and staked my reputation, in a new way. Similarly, saying "I know" is taking a new plunge. But it is *not* saying "I have performed a specially

[15] It is the use of the expressions "I know" and "I promise" (first person singular, present indicative tense) alone that is being considered. "If I knew, I can't have been wrong" or "If she knows she can't be wrong" are not worrying in the way that "If I ('you') know I ('you') can't be wrong" is worrying. Or again, "I promise" is quite different from "he promises": if I say "I promise," I don't say I *say* I promise, I *promise*, just as if he says he promises, he doesn't say he says he promises, he promises: whereas if I say "he promises," I do (only) say he *says* he promises—in the other "sense" of "promise," the "sense" in which *I* say *I* promise, only *he* can say he promises. I *describe* his promising, but I *do* my own promising and he must do *his* own.

striking feat of cognition, superior, in the same scale as believing and being sure, even to being merely quite sure": for there *is* nothing in that scale superior to being quite sure. Just as promising is not something superior, in the same scale as hoping and intending, even to merely fully intending: for there *is* nothing in that scale superior to fully intending. When I say "I know," I *give others my word:* I *give others my authority for saying* that "S is P."

When I have said only that I am sure, and prove to have been mistaken, I am not liable to be rounded on by others in the same way as when I have said "I know." I am sure *for my part,* you can take it or leave it: accept it if you think I'm an acute and careful person, that's your responsibility. But I don't know "for my part," and when I say "I know" I don't mean you can take it or leave it (though of course you *can* take it or leave it). In the same way, when I say I fully intend to, I do so for my part, and, according as you think highly or poorly of my resolution and chances, you will elect to act on it or not to act on it: but if I say I promise, you are *entitled* to act on it, whether or not you choose to do so. If I have said I know or I promise, you insult me in a special way by refusing to accept it. We all *feel* the very great difference between saying even "I'm *absolutely* sure" and saying "I know": it is like the difference between saying even "I firmly and irrevocably intend" and "I promise." If someone has promised me to do A, then I am entitled to rely on it, and can myself make promises on the strength of it: and so, where someone has said to me "I know," I am entitled to say *I* know too, at second hand. The right to say "I know" is transmissible, in the sort of way that other authority is transmissible. Hence, if I say it lightly, I may be *responsible* for getting *you* into trouble.

If you say you *know* something, the most immediate challenge takes the form of asking "Are you in a position to know?": that is, you must undertake to show, not merely that you are sure of it, but that it is within your cognisance. There is a similar form of challenge in the case of promising: fully intending is not enough— you must also undertake to show that "you are in a position to promise," that is, that it is within your power. Over these points in the two cases parallel series of doubts are apt to infect philosophers, on the ground that I canot foresee the future. Some begin to hold that I should never, or practically never, say I know anything—

perhaps only what I am sensing at this moment: others, that I should never, or practically never, say I promise—perhaps only what is actually within my power at this moment. In both cases there is an obsession: if I know *I can't be wrong,* so I can't have the right to say I know, and if I promise *I can't fail,* so I can't have the right to say I promise. And in both cases this obsession fastens on my inability to make *predictions* as the root of the matter, meaning by predictions claims to know the future. But this is doubly mistaken in both cases. As has been seen, we may be perfectly justified in saying we know or we promise, in spite of the fact that things "may" turn out badly, and it's a more or less serious matter for us if they do. And further, it is overlooked that the conditions which must be satisfied if I am to show that a thing is within my cognisance or within my power are conditions, not about the future, but about *the present and the past:* it is not demanded that I do more than *believe* about the future.[16]

We feel, however, an objection to saying that "I know" performs the same sort of function as "I promise." It is this. Supposing that things turn out badly, then we say, on the one hand "You're proved wrong, so you *didn't* know," but on the other hand "You've failed to perform, although you *did* promise." I believe that this contrast is more apparent than real. The sense in which you "did promise" is that you did *say* you promised (did say "I promise"): and you did *say* you knew. That is the gravamen of the charge against you when you let us down, after we have taken your word. But it may well transpire that you never fully intended to do it, or that you had concrete reason to suppose that you wouldn't be able to do it (it might even be manifestly impossible), and in another "sense" of promise you *can't* then have promised to do it, so that you *didn't* promise.

Consider the use of other phrases analogous to "I know" and "I promise." Suppose, instead of "I know," I had said "I swear": in that case, upon the opposite appearing, we should say, exactly as in the promising case, "You *did* swear, but you were wrong." Suppose again that, instead of "I promise," I had said "I guarantee" (*e.g.,* to protect you from attack): in that case, upon my letting you

---

[16] If "Figs never grow on thistles" is taken to mean "None ever have and none ever will," then it is implied that I *know* that none ever have, but only that I *believe* that none ever will.

down, you can say, exactly as in the knowing case "You *said* you guaranteed it, but you *didn't* guarantee it." [17] Can the situation perhaps be summed up as follows? In these "ritual" cases, the approved case is one where *in the appropriate circumstances,* I say a certain formula: for example, "I do" when standing, unmarried or a widower, beside woman, unmarried or a widow and not within the prohibited degrees of relationship, before a clergyman, registrar, and so forth, or "I give" when it is mine to give, and so forth, or "I order" when I have the authority to, and so forth. But now, if the situation transpires to have been in some way not orthodox (I was already married: it wasn't mine to give: I had no authority to order), then we tend to be rather hesitant about how to put it, as heaven was when the saint blessed the penguins. We call the man a bigamist, but his second marriage was not a marriage, is null and void (a useful formula in many cases for avoiding saying either "he did" or "he didn't"): he did "order" me to do it, but, having no authority over me, he *couldn't* "order" me: he did warn me it was going to charge, but it wasn't or anyway I knew much more about it than he did, so in a way he couldn't warn me, didn't warn me.[18] We hesitate between "He didn't order me," "He had no right to order me," "He oughtn't to have said he ordered me," just as we do between "You didn't know," "You can't have known," "You had no right to say you knew" (these perhaps having slightly different nuances, according to what precisely it is that has gone wrong). But the essential factors are (*a*) You said you knew: you said you promised (*b*) You were mistaken: you didn't perform. The hesitancy concerns only the precise way in which we are to round on the original "I know" or "I promise."

To suppose that "I know" is a descriptive phrase, is only one example of the *descriptive fallacy,* so common in philosophy. Even if some language is now purely descriptive, language was not in

---

[17] "Swear," "guarantee," "give my word," "promise," all these and similar words cover cases both of "knowing" and of "promising," thus suggesting the two are analogous. Of course they differ subtly from each other; for example, *know* and *promise* are in a certain sense "unlimited" expressions, while when I swear I swear *upon* something, and when I guarantee I guarantee that, upon some adverse and more or less to be expected circumstance arising, I will take *some more or less definite action* to nullify it.

[18] "You can't warn someone of something that isn't going to happen" parallels "You can't know what isn't true."

origin so, and much of it is still not so. Utterance of obvious ritual phrases, in the appropriate circumstances, is not *describing* the action we are doing, but *doing* it ("I do"): in other cases it functions, like tone and expression, or again like punctuation and mood, as an intimation that we are employing language in some special way ("I warn," "I ask," "I define"). Such phrases cannot, strictly, *be* lies, though they can "imply" lies, as "I promise" implies that I fully intend, which may be untrue.

If these are the main and multifarious points that arise in familiar cases where we ask "How do you know that this is a case of so-and-so?," they may be expected to arise likewise in cases where we say "I know he is angry." And if there are, as no doubt there are, special difficulties in this case, at least we can clear the ground a little of things which are not special difficulties, and get the matter in better perspective.

As a preliminary, it must be said that I shall only discuss the question of feelings and emotions, with special reference to anger. It seems likely that the cases where we know that another man thinks that two and two make four, or that he is seeing a rat, and so on, are different in important respects from, though no doubt also similar to, the case of knowing that he is angry or hungry.

In the first place, we certainly do say sometimes that we know another man is angry, and we also distinguish these occasions from others on which we say only that we *believe* he is angry. For of course, we do not for a moment suppose that we *always* know, of *all* men, whether they are angry or not, or that we could discover it. There are many occasions when I realize that I can't possibly tell what he's feeling: and there are many *types* of people, and many individuals too, with whom I (they being what they are, and I being what I am) never can tell. The feelings of royalty, for example, or fakirs or bushmen or Wykehamists or simple eccentrics—these may be very hard to divine: unless you have had a prolonged acquaintance with such persons, and some intimacy with them, you are not in any sort of position to know what their feelings are, especially if, for one reason or another, they can't or don't tell you. Or again, the feelings of some individual whom you have never met before —they might be almost anything: you don't know his character at all or his tastes, you have had no experience of his mannerisms, and so on. His feelings are elusive and personal: people differ so much. It is this sort of thing that leads to the situation where we say "You never know" or "You never can tell."

In short, here even more than in the case of the goldfinch, a great deal depends on how familiar we have been in our past experience with this type of person, and indeed with this individual, in this type of situation. If we have no great familiarity, then we hesitate to say we know: indeed, we can't be expected to say (tell). On the other hand, if we *have* had the necessary experience, then we can, in favourable current circumstances, say we know: we certainly can recognize when some near relative of ours is angrier than we have ever seen him.

Further, we must have had experience also of the emotion or feeling concerned, in this case anger. In order to know what you are feeling, I must also apparently be able to imagine (guess, understand, appreciate) what you're feeling. It seems that more is demanded than that I shall have learned to discriminate displays of anger in others: I must also have been angry myself.[19] Or at any rate, if I have never felt a certain emotion, say ambition, then I certainly feel an *extra* hesitation in saying that his motive is ambition. And this seems to be due to the very special nature (grammar, logic) of feelings, to the special way in which they are related to their occasions and manifestations, which requires further elucidation.

At first sight it may be tempting to follow Mr. Wisdom, and to draw a distinction between (1) the physical symptoms and (2) the feeling. So that when, in the current case, I am asked "How can you tell he's angry?" I should answer "From the physical symptoms," while if *he* is asked how *he* can tell he's angry, he should answer "From the feeling." But this seems to be a dangerous oversimplification.

In the first place, "symptoms" (and also "physical") is being used

[19] We say we don't know what it must feel like to be a king, whereas we do know what one of our friends must have felt when mortified. In this ordinary (imprecise and evidently not whole-hog) sense of "knowing what it would be like" we do often know what it would be like to be our neighbour drawing his sword, whereas we don't know (can't even guess or imagine), really, what it would feel like to be a cat or a cockroach. But of course we don't ever "know" what in our neighbour accompanies the drawing of his sword in Mr. Wisdom's peculiar sense of "know what" as equivalent to "directly experience that which."

in a way different from ordinary usage, and one which proves to be misleading.

"Symptoms," a term transferred from medical usage,[20] tends to be used only, or primarily, in cases where that of which there are symptoms is something undesirable (of incipient disease rather than of returning health, of despair rather than of hope, of grief rather than of joy): and hence it is more colourful than "signs" or "indications." This, however, is comparatively trivial. What is important is the fact that we never talk of "symptoms" or "signs" except *by way of implied contrast with inspection of the item itself*. No doubt it would often be awkward to have to say exactly where the signs or symptoms end and the item itself begins to appear: but such a division is always implied to exist. And hence the words "symptom" and "sign" have no use except in cases where the item, as in the case of disease, is liable to be *hidden,* whether it be in the future, in the past, under the skin, or in some other more or less notorious casket: and when the item is itself before us, we no longer talk of signs and symptoms. When we talk of "signs of a storm," we mean signs of an impending storm, or of a past storm, or of a storm beyond the horizon: we do *not* mean a storm on top of us.[21]

The words function like such words as "traces" or "clues." Once you know the murderer, you don't get any more clues, only what were or would have been clues: nor is a confession, or an eye witness's view of the crime, a particularly good clue—these are something different altogether. When the cheese is not to be found or seen, then there may be traces of it: but not when it's there in front of us (though of course, there aren't, then, "no traces" of it either).

For this reason, it seems misleading to lump together, as a general practice, all the characteristic features of any casual item as "signs" or "symptoms" of it: though it is of course sometimes the case that some things which could in appropriate circumstances be called

---

[20] Doctors nowadays draw a distinction of their own between "symptoms" and "(physical) signs": but the distinction is not here relevant, and perhaps not very clear.

[21] There are some, more complicated, cases like that of inflation, where the signs of incipient inflation are of the same nature as inflation itself, but of a less intensity or at a slower tempo. Here, especially, it is a matter for decision where the signs or "tendencies" end and where the state itself sets in: moreover, with inflation, as with some diseases, we can in some contexts go on talking of signs or symptoms even when the item itself is quite fairly decidedly present, because it is such as not to be patent to simple observation.

characteristics or effects or manifestations or parts or sequelae or what not of certain items may *also* be called signs or symptoms of those items in the appropriate circumstances. It seems to be this which is really wrong with Mr. Wisdom's paradox (*Other Minds III*) about looking in the larder and finding "all the signs" of bread, when we see the loaf, touch it, taste it and so on. Doing these things is not finding (some) signs of bread at all: the taste or feel of bread is not a sign or symptom of bread at all. What I might be taken to mean if I announced that I had found signs of bread in the larder seems rather doubtful, since bread is not normally casketed (or if in the bin, leaves no traces), and not being a transeunt event (impending bread, *&c.*), does not have any normally accepted "signs": and signs, peculiar to the item, have to be more or less normally accepted. I might be taken to mean that I had found traces of bread, such as crumbs, or signs that bread had at one time been stored there, or something of the kind: but what I could *not* be taken to mean is that I had seen, tasted, or touched (something like) bread.

The sort of thing we do actually say, if the look is all right but we haven't yet tasted it, is "Here is something that looks like bread." If it turns out not to be bread after all, we might say "It tasted like bread, but actually it was only bread substitute," or "It exhibited many of the characteristic features of bread, but differed in important respects: it was only a synthetic imitation." That is, we don't use the words "sign" or "symptom" at all.

Now, if "signs" and "symptoms" have this restricted usage, it is evident that to say that we only get at the "signs" or "symptoms" of anything is to imply that we never get at *it* (and this goes for "*all* the signs" too). So that, if we say that I only get at the *symptoms* of his anger, that carries an important implication. But *is* this the way we do talk? Surely we do not consider that we are never aware of more than *symptoms* of anger in another man?

"Symptoms" or "signs" of anger tend to mean signs of *rising* or of *suppressed* anger. Once the man has exploded, we talk of something different—of an expression or manifestation or display of anger, of an exhibition of temper, and so forth. A twitch of the eyebrow, pallor, a tremor in the voice, all these may be symptoms of anger: but a violent tirade or a blow in the face are not, they are the acts in which the anger is vented. "Symptoms" of anger are not, at least normally, contrasted with the man's own inner personal feeling of anger, but rather with the actual display of anger. Normally at least, where we have only symptoms to go upon, we should say only that we *believe* that the man is angry or getting angry: whereas when he has given himself away we say that we *know*.[22]

The word "physical" also, as used by Mr. Wisdom in contrast to "mental," seems to me abused, though I am not confident as to whether this abuse is misleading in the current case. He evidently does not wish to call a man's feelings, which he cites as a typical example of a "mental" event, *physical*. Yet this is what we ordinarily often do. There are many physical feelings, such as giddiness, hunger or fatigue: and these are included by some doctors among the physical signs of various complaints. Most feelings we do not speak of as either mental or physical, especially emotions, such as jealousy or anger itself: we do not assign them to the *mind* but to the *heart*. Where we do describe a feeling as mental, it is because we are using a word normally used to describe a physical feeling in a special transferred sense, as when we talk about "mental" discomfort or fatigue.

It is then, clear, that more is involved in being, for example, angry than simply showing the symptoms and feeling the feeling. For there is also the display or manifestation. And it is to be noted that the feeling is related in a unique sort of way to the display. When we are angry, we have an impulse, felt and/or acted on, to do actions of particular kinds, and, unless we suppress the anger, we do actually proceed to do them. There is a peculiar and intimate relationship between the emotion and the natural manner of venting it, with which, having been angry ourselves, we are acquainted. The ways in which anger is normally manifested are *natural* to anger just as there are tones *naturally* expressive of various emotions

[22] Sometimes, it is said, we use "I know" where we should be prepared to substitute "I believe," as when we say "I know he's in, because his hat is in the hall": "I know" is used loosely for "believe," so why should we suppose there is a fundamental difference between them? But the question is, what exactly do we mean by "prepared to substitute" and "loosely"? We are "prepared to substitute" *believe* for *know* not as an *equivalent* expression but as a weaker and therefore preferable expression, in view of the seriousness with which, as has become apparent, the matter is to be treated: the presence of the hat, which would serve as a proof of its owner's presence in many circumstances, could only through laxity be adduced as a proof in a court of law.

(indignation, &c.). There is not normally taken to be[23] such a thing as "being angry" apart from any impulse, however vague, to vent the anger in the natural way.

Moreover, besides the natural expressions of anger, there are also the natural *occasions* of anger, of which we have also had experience, which are similarly connected in an intimate way with the "being angry." It would be as nonsensical to class these as "causes" in some supposedly obvious and "external" sense, as it would be to class the venting of anger as the "effect" of the emotion in a supposedly obvious and "external" sense. Equally it would be nonsensical to say that there are three wholly distinct phenomena, (1) cause or occasion, (2) feeling or emotion, and (3) effect or manifestation, which are related together "by definition" as all necessary to anger, though this would perhaps be less misleading than the other.

It seems fair to say that "being angry" is in many respects like "having mumps." It is a description of a whole pattern of events, including occasion, symptoms, feeling and manifestation, and possibly other factors besides. It is as silly to ask "What, really, *is* the anger *itself?*" as to attempt to fine down "the disease" to some one chosen item ("the functional disorder"). That the man himself feels something which we don't (in the sense that he feels angry and we don't) is, in the absence of Mr. Wisdom's variety of telepathy,[24] evident enough, and incidentally nothing to complain about as a "predicament": but there is no call to say that "that" ("the feeling")[25] *is* the *anger*. The pattern of events whatever its precise form, is, fairly clearly, peculiar to the case of "feelings" (emotions)—it is not by any means exactly like the case of diseases: and it seems to be this peculiarity which makes us prone to say that, unless we have

---

[23] A new language is naturally necessary if we are to admit unconscious feelings, and feelings which express themselves in paradoxical manners, such as the psychoanalysts describe.

[24] There is, it seems to me, something which does actually happen, rather different from Mr. Wisdom's telepathy, which does sometimes contribute towards our knowledge of other people's feelings. We do talk, for example, of "feeling another person's displeasure," and say, for example, "his anger could be felt," and there seems to be something genuine about this. But the feeling we feel, though a genuine "feeling," is *not*, in these cases, displeasure or anger, but a special *counterpart* feeling.

[25] The "feelings," *i.e.*, sensations, we can observe in ourselves when angry are such things as a pounding of the heart or tensing of the muscles, which cannot in themselves be justifiably called "the feeling of anger."

had experience of a feeling ourselves, we cannot know when someone else is experiencing it. Moreover, it is our confidence in the
general pattern that makes us apt to say we "know" another man
is angry when we have only observed parts of the pattern: for the
parts of the pattern are related to each other very much more intimately than, for example, newspapermen scurrying in Brighton
are related to a fire in Fleet Street.[26]

The man himself, such is the overriding power of the pattern,
will sometimes accept corrections from outsiders about his own
emotions, that is, about the correct description of them. He may
be got to agree that he was not really angry so much as, rather,
indignant or jealous, and even that he was not in pain, but only
fancied he was. And this is not surprising, especially in view of the
fact that he, like all of us, has primarily learnt to use the expression
"I am angry" of himself by (a) noting the occasion, symptoms, manifestation, and so forth, in cases where other persons say "I am
angry" of *themselves* (b) being told by others, who have noted all
that can be observed about *him* on certain occasions, that "You are
angry," that is, that he should say "I am angry." On the whole,
"mere" feelings or emotions, if there are such things genuinely
detectable, are certainly very hard to be sure about, even harder
than, say, tastes, which we already choose to describe, normally,
only by their occasions (the taste "of tar," "of pineapple," &c.).

All words for emotions are, besides, on the vague side, in two
ways, leading to further hesitations about whether we "know" when
he's angry. They tend to cover a rather wide and ill-defined variety
of situations: and the patterns they cover tend to be, each of them,
rather complex (though common and so not difficult to recognize,
very often), so that it is easy for one of the more or less necessary
features to be omitted, and thus to give rise to hesitation about what
exactly we should say in such an unorthodox case. We realize, well
enough, that the challenge to which we are exposed if we say we
know is to *prove* it, and in this respect vagueness of terminology is
a crippling handicap.

So far, enough has perhaps been said to show that most of the
difficulties which stand in the way of our saying we know a thing
is a goldfinch arise in rather greater strength in the case where we

[26] It is therefore misleading to ask "How do I get from the scowl to the
anger?"

want to say we know another man is angry. But there is still a feeling, and I think a justified feeling, that there is a further and quite *special* difficulty in the latter case.

This difficulty seems to be of the sort that Mr. Wisdom raises at the very outset of his series of articles on "Other Minds." It is asked, might the man not exhibit all the symptoms (and display and everything else) of anger, even ad infinitum, and yet still *not* (*really*) *be* angry? It will be remembered that he there treats it, no doubt provisionally, as a difficulty similar to that which can arise concerning the reality of any "material object." But in fact, it has special features of its own.

There seem to be three distinguishable doubts which may arise:

(1) When to all appearances angry, might he not really be labouring under some other emotion, in that, though he normally feels the same emotion as we should on occasions when we, in his position, should feel anger and in making displays such as we make when angry, in this particular case he is acting abnormally?

(2) When to all appearances angry, might he not really be labouring under some other emotion, in that he normally feels, on occasions when we in his position should feel anger and when acting as we should act if we felt anger, some feeling which we, if we experienced it, should distinguish from anger?

(3) When to all appearances angry, might he not really be feeling no emotion at all?

In everyday life, all these problems arise in special cases, and occasion genuine worry. We may worry (1) as to whether someone is *deceiving* us, by suppressing his emotions, or by feigning emotions which he does not feel: we may worry (2) as to whether we are *misunderstanding* someone (or he us), in wrongly supposing that he does "feel like us," that he does share emotions like ours: or we may worry (3) as to whether some action of another person is really deliberate, or perhaps only involuntary or inadvertent in some manner or other. All three varieties of worry may arise, and often do, in connexion with the actions of persons whom we know very well.[27] Any or all of them may be at the bottom of the passage

[27] There is, too, a special way in which we can doubt the "reality" of our own emotions, can doubt whether we are not "acting to ourselves." Professional actors may reach a state where they never really know what their genuine feelings are.

from Mrs. Woolf:[28] all work together in the feeling of loneliness which affects everybody at times.

None of these three special difficulties about "reality" arises in connexion with goldfinches or bread, any more than the special difficulties about, for example, the oasis arise in connexion with the reality of another person's emotions. The goldfinch cannot be assumed, nor the bread suppressed: we may be deceived by the appearance of an oasis, or misinterpret the signs of the weather, but the oasis cannot lie to us and we cannot misunderstand the storm in the way we misunderstand the man.

Though the difficulties are special, the ways of dealing with them are, initially, similar to those employed in the case of the goldfinch. There are (more or less roughly) established procedures for dealing with suspected cases of deception or of misunderstanding or of inadvertence. By these means we do very often establish (though we do not expect *always* to establish) that someone is acting, or that we were misunderstanding him, or that he is simply impervious to a certain emotion, or that he was not acting voluntarily. These special cases where doubts arise and require resolving, are contrasted with the normal cases which hold the field [29] *unless* there is some special suggestion that deceit, and so forth, is involved, and deceit, moreover, of an intelligible kind in the circumstances, that is, of a kind that can be looked into because motive, and so forth, is specially suggested. There is no suggestion that I *never* know what other people's emotions are, nor yet that in particular cases I might be wrong for no special reason or in no special way.

Extraordinary cases of deceit, misunderstanding, and so forth (which are themselves not the normal), do not, *ex vi termini*, ordinarily occur: we have a working knowledge of the occasions for, the temptations to, the practical limits of, and the normal types of deceit and misunderstanding. Nevertheless, they *may* occur, and there may be varieties which are common without our yet having become aware of the fact. If this happens, we are in a certain sense wrong, because our terminology is inadequate to the facts, and we shall have thenceforward to be more wary about saying we know, or shall have

---

[28] [Quoted by Wisdom in his contribution to this Symposium.—Editor]

[29] "You cannot fool all of the people all of the time" is "analytic."

to revise our ideas and terminology. This we are constantly ready to do in a field so complex and baffling as that of the emotions.

There remains, however, one further special feature of the case, which also differentiates it radically from the goldfinch case. The goldfinch, the material object, is, as we insisted above, uninscribed and *mute:* but the man *speaks.* In the complex of occurrences which induces us to say we know another man is angry, the complex of symptoms, occasion, display, and the rest, a peculiar place is occupied by the man's own statement as to what his feelings are. In the usual case, we accept this statement without question, and we then say that we know (as it were "at secondhand") what his feelings are: though of course "at secondhand" here could not be used to imply that anybody but he could know "at firsthand," and hence perhaps it is not in fact used. In unusual cases, where his statement conflicts with the description we should otherwise have been inclined to give of the case, we do not feel bound to accept it, though we always feel some uneasiness in rejecting it. If the man is an habitual liar or self-deceiver, or if there are patent reasons why he should be lying or deceiving himself on this occasion, then we feel reasonably happy: but if such a case occurred as the imagined one where a man, having given throughout life every appearance of holding a certain pointless belief, leaves behind a remark in his private diary to the effect that he never did believe it, then we probably should not know what to say.

I should like to make in conclusion some further remarks about this crucial matter of our believing what the man says about his own feelings. Although I know very well that I do not see my way clearly in this, I cannot help feeling sure that it is fundamental to the whole Predicament, and that it has not been given the attention it deserves, possibly just because it is so obvious.

The man's own statement is not (is not treated primarily as) a sign or symptom, although it can, secondarily and artificially, be treated as such. A unique place is reserved for it in the summary of the facts of the case. The question then is: "Why believe him?"

There are answers that we can give to this question, which is here to be taken in the general sense of "Why believe him ever?" not simply as "Why believe him this time?" We may say that the man's statements on matters other than his own feelings have constantly been before us in the past, and have been regularly verified by our own observations of the facts he reported: so that we have in fact some basis for an induction about his general reliability. Or we may say that his behaviour is most simply "explained" on the view that he does feel emotions like ours, just as psychoanalysts "explain" erratic behaviour by analogy with normal behaviour when they use the terminology of "unconscious desires."

These answers are, however, dangerous and unhelpful. They are so obvious that they please nobody: while on the other hand they encourage the questioner to push his question to "profounder" depths, encouraging us, in turn, to exaggerate these answers until they become distortions.

The question, pushed further, becomes a challenge to the very possibility of "believing another man," in its ordinarily accepted sense, at all. What "justification" is there for supposing that there is another mind communicating with you at all? How can you know what it would be like for another mind to feel anything, and so how can you understand it? It is then that we are tempted to say that we only mean by "believing him" that we take certain vocal noises as signs of certain impending behaviour, and that "other minds" are no more really real than unconscious desires.

This, however, is distortion. It seems, rather, that believing in other persons, in authority and testimony, is an essential part of the act of communicating, an act which we all constantly perform. It is as much an irreducible part of our experience as, say, giving promises, or playing competitive games, or even sensing coloured patches. We can state certain advantages of such performances, and we can elaborate rules of a kind for their "rational" conduct (as the Law Courts and historians and psychologists work out the rules for accepting testimony). But there is no "justification" for our doing them as such.

FINAL NOTE

One speaker at Manchester said roundly that the real crux of the matter remains still that "I ought not to say that I know Tom is angry, because I don't introspect his feelings": and this no doubt is just what many people do boggle at. The gist of what I have been trying to bring out is simply:

(1) *Of course* I *don't* introspect Tom's feelings (we should be in a pretty predicament if I did).

(2) *Of course* I *do* sometimes know Tom is angry.
Hence

(3) to suppose that the question "How do I know that Tom is angry?" is meant to mean "How do I introspect Tom's feelings?" (because, as we know, that's the sort of thing that knowing is or ought to be), is simply barking our way up the wrong gum tree.

W. V. QUINE

The Basis of Conceptual Schemes

~~~~~~

POSITS AND REALITY

I. Subvisible Particles

According to physics my desk is, for all its seeming fixity and solidity, a swarm of vibrating molecules. The desk as we sense it is comparable to a distant haystack in which we cannot distinguish the individual stalks; comparable also to a wheel in which, because of its rapid rotation, we cannot distinguish the individual spokes. Comparable, but with a difference. By approaching the haystack we can distinguish the stalks, and by retarding the wheel we can distinguish the spokes. On the other hand no glimpse is to be had of the separate molecules of the desk; they are, we are told, too small.

Lacking such experience, what evidence can the physicist muster for his doctrine of molecules? His answer is that there is a convergence of indirect evidence, drawn from such varied phenomena as expansion, heat conduction, capillary attraction, and surface tension. The point is that these miscellaneous phenomena can, if we assume the molecular theory, be marshaled under the familiar laws of motion. The fancifulness of thus assuming a substructure of moving particles of imperceptible size is offset by a gain in

* The first selection is Quine's article "Posits and Reality" from S. Uyeda, editor, *Basis of Contemporary Philosophy* (Tokyo: Waseda University Press, 1960); it is reprinted by permission of the author and the publisher. The second consists of the sixth section of Quine's "Two Dogmas of Empiricism," *The Philosophical Review* 1951; it is reprinted by permission of the editors and the author.

naturalness and scope on the part of the aggregate laws of physics. The molecular theory is felt, moreover, to gain corroboration progressively as the physicist's predictions of future observations turn out to be fulfilled, and as the theory proves to invite extensions covering additional classes of phenomena.

The benefits thus credited to the molecular doctrine may be divided into five. One is simplicity: empirical laws concerning seemingly dissimilar phenomena are integrated into a compact and unitary theory. Another is familiarity of principle: the already familiar laws of motion are made to serve where independent laws would otherwise have been needed. A third is scope: the resulting unitary theory implies a wider array of testable consequences than any likely accumulation of separate laws would have implied. A fourth is fecundity: successful further extensions of theory are expedited. The fifth goes without saying: such testable consequences of the theory as have been tested have turned out well, aside from such sparse exceptions as may in good conscience be chalked up to unexplained interferences.

Simplicity, the first of the listed benefits, is a vague business. We may be fairly sure of this much: theories are more or less simple, more or less unitary, only relative to one or another given vocabulary or conceptual apparatus. Simplicity is, if not quite subjective, at any rate parochial. Yet simplicity contributes to scope, as follows. An empirical theory, typically, generalizes or extrapolates from sample data, and thus covers more phenomena than have been checked. Simplicity, by our lights, is what guides our extrapolation. Hence the simpler the theory, on the whole, the wider this unchecked coverage.

As for the fourth benefit, fecundity, obviously it is a consequence of the first two, simplicity and familiarity, for these two traits are the best conditions for effective thinking.

Not all the listed benefits are generally attributable to accepted scientific theories, though all are to be prized when available. Thus the benefit of familiarity of principle may, as in quantum theory and relativity theory, be renounced, its loss being regretted but outweighed.

But to get back. In its manifest content the molecular doctrine bears directly on unobservable reality, affirming a structure of minute swarming particles. On the other hand any defense of it has to do rather with its indirect bearing on observable reality. The doctrine has this indirect bearing by being the core of an integrated physical theory which implies truth about expansion, conduction, and so on. The benefits which we have been surveying are benefits which the molecular doctrine, as core, brings to the physics of these latter observable phenomena.

Suppose now we were to excise that core but retain the surrounding ring of derivative laws, thus not disturbing the observable consequences. The retained laws could be viewed thenceforward as autonomous empirical laws, innocent of any molecular commitment. Granted, this combination of empirical laws would never have been achieved without the unifying aid of a molecular doctrine at the center; note the recent remarks on scope. But we might still delete the molecular doctrine once it has thus served its heuristic purpose.

This reflection strengthens a natural suspicion: that the benefits conferred by the molecular doctrine give the physicist good reason to prize it, but afford no evidence of its truth. Though the doctrine succeed to perfection in its indirect bearing on observable reality, the question of its truth has to do rather with its direct claim on unobservable reality. Might the molecular doctrine not be ever so useful in organizing and extending our knowledge of the behavior of observable things, and yet be factually false?

One may question, on closer consideration, whether this is really an intelligible possibility. Let us reflect upon our words and how we learned them.

II. Posits and Analogies

Words are human artifacts, meaningless save as our associating them with experience endows them with meaning. The word "swarm" is initially meaningful to us through association with such experiences as that of a hovering swarm of gnats, or a swarm of dust moles in a shaft of sunlight. When we extend the word to desks and the like, we are engaged in drawing an analogy between swarms ordinarily so-called, on the one hand, and desks, and so forth, on the other. The word "molecule" is then given meaning derivatively: having conceived of desks analogically as swarms, we imagine molecules as the things the desks are swarms of.

The purported question of fact, the question whether the familiar objects around us are really swarms of subvisible particles in vibration, now begins to waver and dissolve. If the words involved here make sense only by analogy, then the only question of fact is the question how good an analogy there is between the behavior of a desk or the like and the behavior, for example, of a swarm of gnats. What had seemed a direct bearing of the molecular doctrine upon reality has now dwindled to an analogy.

Even this analogical content, moreover, is incidental, variable, and at length dispensable. In particular the analogy between the swarming of the molecules of a solid and the swarming of gnats is only moderately faithful; a supplementary aid to appreciating the dynamics of the molecules of a solid is found in the analogy of a stack of bedsprings. In another and more recondite part of physics, the theory of light, the tenuousness of analogy is notorious: the analogy of particles is useful up to a point and the analogy of waves is useful up to a point, but neither suffices to the exclusion of the other. Faithful analogies are an aid to the physicist's early progress in an unaccustomed medium, but, like water wings, they are an aid which he learns to get along without.

In Section I we contrasted a direct and an indirect bearing of the molecular doctrine upon reality. But the direct bearing has not withstood scrutiny. Where there had at first seemed to be an undecidable question of unobservable fact, we now find mere analogy at most and not necessarily that. So the only way in which we now find the molecular doctrine genuinely to bear upon reality is the indirect way, via implications in observable phenomena.

The effect of this conclusion upon the status of molecules is that they lose even the dignity of inferred or hypothetical entities which may or may not really be there. The very sentences which seem to propound them and treat of them are gibberish by themselves, and indirectly significant only as contributory clauses of an inclusive system which does also treat of the real. The molecular physicist is, like all of us, concerned with commonplace reality, and merely finds that he can simplify his laws by positing an esoteric supplement to the exoteric universe. He can devise simpler laws for this enriched universe, this "sesquiverse" of his own decree, than he has been able to devise for its real or original portion alone.

In Section I we imagined deleting the molecular doctrine from the midst of the derivative body of physical theory. From our present vantage point, however, we see that operation as insignificant; there is no substantive doctrine of molecules to delete. The sentences which seem to propound molecules are just devices for organizing the significant sentences of physical theory. No matter if physics makes molecules or other insensible particles seem more fundamental than the objects of common sense; the particles are posited for the sake of a simple physics.

The tendency of our own reflections has been, conversely, to belittle molecules and their ilk, leaving common-sense bodies supreme. Still, it may now be protested, this invidious contrast is unwarranted. What are given in sensation are variformed and varicolored visual patches, varitextured and varitemperatured tactual feels, and an assortment of tones, tastes, smells, and other odds and ends; desks are no more to be found among these data than molecules. If we have evidence for the existence of the bodies of common sense, we have it only in the way in which we may be said to have evidence for the existence of molecules. The positing of either sort of body is good science insofar merely as it helps us formulate our laws—laws whose ultimate evidence lies in the sense data of the past, and whose ultimate vindication lies in anticipation of sense data of the future. The positing of molecules differs from the positing of the bodies of common sense mainly in degree of sophistication. In whatever sense the molecules in my desk are unreal and a figment of the imagination of the scientist, in that sense the desk itself is unreal and a figment of the imagination of the race.

This double verdict of unreality leaves us nothing, evidently, but the raw sense data themselves. It leaves each of us, indeed, nothing but his own sense data; for the assumption of there being other persons has no better support than has the assumption of there being any other sorts of external objects. It leaves each of us in the position of solipsism, according to which there is nobody else in the world, nor indeed any world but the pageant of one's own sense data.

III. Restitution

Surely now we have been caught up in a wrong line of reasoning. Not only is the conclusion bizarre; it vitiates the very considerations that lead to it. We cannot properly represent man as inventing a myth of physical objects to fit past and present sense data, for past ones are lost except to memory; and memory, far from being a straightforward register of past sense data, usually depends on past posits of physical objects. The positing of physical objects must be seen not as an *ex post facto* systematization of data, but as a move prior to which no appreciable data would be available to systematize.

Something went wrong with our standard of reality. We became doubtful of the reality of molecules because the physicist's statement that there are molecules took on the aspect of a mere technical convenience in smoothing the laws of physics. Next we noted that common-sense bodies are epistemologically much on a par with the molecules, and inferred the unreality of the common-sense bodies themselves. Here our bemusement becomes visible. Unless we change meanings in midstream, the familiar bodies around us are as real as can be; and it smacks of a contradiction in terms to conclude otherwise. Having noted that man has no evidence for the existence of bodies beyond the fact that their assumption helps him organize experience, we should have done well, instead of disclaiming evidence for the existence of bodies, to conclude: such, then, at bottom, is what evidence is, both for ordinary bodies and for molecules.

This point about evidence does not upset the evidential priority of sense data. On the contrary, the point about evidence is precisely that the testimony of the senses *does* (contrary to Berkeley's notion) count as evidence for bodies, such being (as Samuel Johnson perceived) just the sort of thing that evidence is. We can continue to recognize, as in Section II, that molecules and even the gross bodies of common sense are simply posited in the course of organizing our responses to stimulation; but a moral to draw from our reconsideration of the terms "reality" and "evidence" is that posits are not *ipso facto* unreal. The benefits of the molecular doctrine which so impressed us in Section I, and the manifest benefits of the aboriginal posit of ordinary bodies, are the best evidence of reality we can ask (pending, of course, evidence of the same sort for some alternative ontology).

Sense data are posits too. They are posits of psychological theory, but not, on that account, unreal. The sense datum may be construed as a hypothetical component of subjective experience standing in closest possible correspondence to the experimentally measurable conditions of physical stimulation of the end organs. In seeking to isolate sense data we engage in empirical psychology, associating physical stimuli with human resources. I shall not guess how useful the positing of sense data may be for psychological theory, or more specifically for a psychologically grounded theory of evidence, nor what detailed traits may profitably be postulated concerning them. In our flight from the fictitious to the real, in any event, we have come full circle.

Sense data, if they are to be posited at all, are fundamental in one respect; the small particles of physics are fundamental in a second respect, and common-sense bodies in a third. Sense data are *evidentially* fundamental: every man is beholden to his senses for every hint of bodies. The physical particles are *naturally* fundamental, in this kind of way: laws of behavior of those particles afford, so far as we know, the simplest formulation of a general theory of what happens. Common-sense bodies, finally, are *conceptually* fundamental; it is by reference to them that the very notions of reality and evidence are acquired, and that the concepts which have to do with physical particles or even with sense data tend to be framed and phrased. But these three types of priority must not be viewed as somehow determining three competing, self-sufficient conceptual schemes. Our one serious conceptual scheme is the inclusive, evolving one of science, which we inherit and, in our several small ways, help to improve.

IV. Working from Within

It is by thinking within this unitary conceptual scheme itself, thinking about the process of the physical world, that we come to appreciate that the world can be evidenced only through stimulation of our senses. It is by thinking within the same conceptual scheme that we come to appreciate that language, being a social art, is learned primarily with reference to intersubjectively conspicuous objects, and hence that such objects are bound to be central conceptually. Both of these *aperçus* are part of the scientific understanding of the scientific enterprise; not prior to it. Insofar as they help the scientist to proceed more knowingly about his business, science is using its findings to improve its own techniques. Epistemology, on this view, is not logically prior somehow to common sense or to the refined common sense which is science; it is part rather of the overall scientific enterprise, an enterprise which Neurath has likened to that of rebuilding a ship while staying afloat in it.

Epistemology, so conceived, continues to probe the sensory evidence for discourse about the world; but it no longer seeks to relate such discourse somehow to an imaginary and impossible sense-datum language. Rather it faces the fact that society teaches us our physicalistic language by training us to associate various physicalistic sentences directly, in multifarious ways, with irritations of our sensory surfaces, and by training us also to associate various such sentences with one another.

The complex totality of such associations is a fluctuating field of force. Some sentences about bodies are, for one person or for many, firmly conditioned one by one to sensory stimulation of specifiable sorts. Roughly specifiable sequences of nerve hits can confirm us in statements about having had breakfast, or there being a brick house on Elm Street, beyond the power of secondary associations with other sentences to add or detract. But there is in this respect a grading-off from one example to another. Many sentences even about common-sense bodies rest wholly on indirect evidence; witness the statement that one of the pennies now in my pocket was in my pocket last week. Conversely, sentences even about electrons are sometimes directly conditioned to sensory stimulation, for example, via the cloud chamber. The status of a given sentence, in point of direct or indirect connection with the senses, can change as one's experience accumulates; thus a man's first confrontation with a cloud chamber may forge a direct sensory link to some sentences which hitherto bore, for him, only the most indirect sensory relevance. Moreover the sensory relevance of sentences will differ widely from person to person; uniformity comes only where the pressure for communication comes.

Statements about bodies, common-sense or recondite, thus commonly make little or no empirical sense except as bits of a collectively significant containing system. Various statements can surely be supplanted by their negations, without conflict with any possible sensory contingency, provided that we revise other portions of our science in compensatory ways. Science is empirically underdetermined: there is slack. What can be said about the hypothetical particles of physics is *underdetermined* by what can be said about sensible bodies, and what can be said about these is underdetermined by the stimulation of our surfaces. An inkling of this circumstance has doubtless fostered the tendency to look upon the hypothetical particles of physics as more of a fiction than sensible bodies, and these as more of a fiction than sense data. But the tendency is a perverse one, for it ascribes full reality only to a domain of objects for which there is no autonomous system of discourse at all.

Better simply to explore, realistically, the less-than-rigid connections that obtain between sensory stimulus and physical doctrine, without viewing this want of rigidity as impugning the physical doctrine. Benefits of the sort recounted in Section I are what count for the molecular doctrine or any, and we can hope for no surer touchstone of reality. We can hope to improve our physics by seeking the same sorts of benefits in fuller measure, and we may even facilitate such endeavors by better understanding the degrees of freedom that prevail between stimulatory evidence and physical doctrine. But as a medium for such epistemological inquiry we can choose no better than the selfsame world theory which we are trying to improve, this being the best available at the time.

EMPIRICISM WITHOUT DOGMAS

The totality of our so-called knowledge or beliefs, from the most casual matters of geography and history to the profoundest laws of atomic physics or even of pure mathematics and logic, is a man-made fabric which impinges on experience only along the edges. Or, to change the figure, total science is like a field of force whose boundary conditions are experience. A conflict with experience at the periphery occasions readjustments in the interior of the field. Truth values have to be redistributed over some of our statements. Reevaluation of some statements entails reevaluation of others, because of their logical interconnections—the logical laws being in turn simply certain further statements of the system, certain further elements of the field. Having reevaluated one statement we must reevaluate some others, which may be the statements logically connected with the first or may be the statements of logical connections themselves. But the total field is so underdetermined by its boundary conditions, experience, that there is much latitude of choice as to what statements to reevaluate in the light of any single contrary experience. No particular experiences are linked with any particular statements in the interior of the field, except indirectly through considerations of equilibrium affecting the field as a whole.

If this view is right, it is misleading to speak of the empirical content of an individual statement—especially if it is a statement at all remote from the experiential periphery of the field. Furthermore it becomes folly to seek a boundary between synthetic statements, which hold contingently on experience, and analytic statements, which hold come what may. Any statement can be held true come what may, if we make drastic enough adjustments elsewhere in the system. Even a statement very close to the periphery can be held true in the face of recalcitrant experience by pleading hallucination or by amending certain statements of the kind called logical laws. Conversely, by the same token, no statement is immune to revision. Revision even of the logical law of the excluded middle has been proposed as a means of simplifying quantum mechanics; and what difference is there in principle between such a shift and the shift whereby Kepler superseded Ptolemy, or Einstein Newton, or Darwin Aristotle?

For vividness I have been speaking in terms of varying distances from a sensory periphery. Let me try now to clarify this notion without metaphor. Certain statements, though *about* physical objects and not sense experience, seem peculiarly germane to sense experience—and in a selective way: some statements to some experiences, others to others. Such statements, especially germane to particular experiences, I picture as near the periphery. But in this relation of "germaneness" I envisage nothing more than a loose association reflecting the relative likelihood, in practice, of our choosing one statement rather than another for revision in the event of recalcitrant experience. For example, we can imagine recalcitrant experiences to which we would surely be inclined to accommodate our system by reevaluating just the statement that there are brick houses on Elm Street, together with related statements on the same topic. We can imagine other recalcitrant experiences to which we would be inclined to accommodate our system by reevaluating just the statement that there are no centaurs, along with kindred statements. A recalcitrant experience can, I have urged, be accommodated by any of various alternative reevaluations in various alternative quarters of the total system; but, in the cases which we are now imagining, our natural tendency to disturb the total system as little as possible would lead us to focus our revisions upon these specific statements concerning brick houses or centaurs. These statements are felt, therefore, to have a sharper empirical reference than highly theoretical statements of physics or logic or ontology. The latter statements may be thought of as relatively centrally located within the total network, meaning merely that little preferential connection with any particular sense data obtrudes itself.

As an empiricist I continue to think of the conceptual scheme of science as a tool, ultimately, for predicting future experience in the light of past experience. Physical objects are conceptually imported into the situation as convenient intermediaries—not by definition in terms of experience, but simply as irreducible posits comparable, epistemologically, to the gods of Homer. For my part I do, qua lay physicist, believe in physical objects and not in Homer's gods; and I consider it a scientific error to believe otherwise. But in point of epistemological footing the physical objects and the gods differ only in degree and not in kind. Both sorts of entities enter our conception only as cultural posits. The myth of physical objects is epistemologically superior to most in that it has proved more efficacious than other myths as a device for working a manageable structure into the flux of experience.

Positing does not stop with macroscopic physical objects. Objects at the atomic level are posited to make the laws of macroscopic objects, and ultimately the laws of experience, simpler and more manageable; and we need not expect or demand full definition of atomic and subatomic entities in terms of macroscopic ones, any more than definition of macroscopic things in terms of sense data. Science is a continuation of common sense, and it continues the commonsense expedient of swelling ontology to simplify theory.

Physical objects, small and large, are not the only posits. Forces are another example; and indeed we are told nowadays that the boundary between energy and matter is obsolete. Moreover, the abstract entities which are the substance of mathematics—ultimately classes and classes of classes and so on up—are another posit in the same spirit. Epistemologically these are myths on the same footing with physical objects and gods, neither better nor worse except for differences in the degree to which they expedite our dealings with sense experiences.

The overall algebra of rational and irrational numbers is underdetermined by the algebra of rational numbers, but is smoother and more convenient; and it includes the algebra of rational numbers as a jagged or gerrymandered part. Total science, mathematical and natural and human, is similarly but more extremely underdetermined by experience. The edge of the system must be kept squared with experience; the rest, with all its elaborate myths or fictions, has as its objective the simplicity of laws.

Ontological questions, under this view, are on a par with questions of natural science. Consider the question whether to countenance classes as entities. This, as I have argued elsewhere, is the question whether to quantify with respect to variables which take classes as values. Now Carnap has maintained that this is a question not of matters of fact but of choosing a convenient language form, a convenient conceptual scheme or framework for science. With this I agree, but only on the proviso that the same be conceded regarding scientific hypotheses generally. Carnap has recognized that he is able to preserve a double standard for ontological questions and scientific hypotheses only by assuming an absolute distinction between the analytic and the synthetic; and I need not say again that this is a distinction which I reject.

The issue over there being classes seems more a question of convenient conceptual scheme; the issue over there being centaurs, or brick houses on Elm Street, seems more a question of fact. But I have been urging that this difference is only one of degree, and that it turns upon our vaguely pragmatic inclination to adjust one strand of the fabric of science rather than another in accommodating some particular recalcitrant experience. Conservatism figures in such choices, and so does the quest for simplicity.

Carnap, Lewis, and others take a pragmatic stand on the question of choosing between language forms, scientific frameworks; but their pragmatism leaves off at the imagined boundary between the analytic and the synthetic. In repudiating such a boundary I espouse a more thorough pragmatism. Each man is given a scientific heritage plus a continuing barrage of sensory stimulation; and the considerations which guide him in warping his scientific heritage to fit his continuing sensory promptings are, where rational, pragmatic.

NELSON GOODMAN

Sense and Certainty

The argument for empirical certainties has two phases. The first is
the effort to point out actual statements or kinds of statements that
are plainly immune to doubt. The second is the effort to show, quite
aside from the question just *what* statements are certain, that on
theoretical grounds there must be *some* empirical certainties.

The popular hunting ground for empirical certainty is among
statements confined to immediate phenomena. Statements concerning physical objects involve prediction in one way or another, and
so may always turn out to be wrong. But, the argument runs, between the presentation of an element in experience and my simultaneous judgment that it is presented, there is no room for error
or doubt. We may have trouble formulating these judgments correctly in language, but misuses of language or slips of tongue must
not be confused with errors in judgment. If the judgment is immediate and confined to what is fully before me, it cannot be wrong.
For how can I be mistaken at a given moment about the sheer
content of my experience at that moment?

Despite the forthright appeal of this argument, the fact seems to
be that my judgments at a moment about what I immediately
apprehend at that moment are often wrong. That is to say, they
are often withdrawn for good reason. This is sometimes denied on
the ground that, since the momentary experience is instantly gone,
the judgment is forever safe from further test. But the judgment

* Reprinted from *The Philosophical Review* 1952 with the permission of the
editors and the author.

I made a few moments ago that a reddish patch occupied the center of my visual field at that moment will be dropped if it conflicts with other judgments having a combined stronger claim to preservation. For example, if I also judged that the patch occupying the same region an instant later was blue, and also that the apparent color was constant over the brief period covering the two instants, I am going to have to drop one of the three judgments; and circumstances may point to the first as well as to either of the others. Indeed judgments concerning immediate phenomena may be rejected in favor of judgments concerning physical objects, as happens when I conclude that it could not have been a reddish patch after all since I was looking at a bluebird in sunlight with my eyes functioning normally. In either sort of case, I cannot reasonably plead a mere slip of the tongue; I am deciding that a judgment was wrong. If a statement may be withdrawn in the interest of compatibility and other statements, it is not certain in any ordinary sense; for certainty consists of immunity to such withdrawal.

Now someone may object that all I have shown is that a judgment concerning phenomena at a given moment may be doubted at some later moment, while what is being claimed is merely that such a judgment is certain *at* the moment in question. This seems to me a confusion. When we talk of certainty we are not—I take it—talking about a feeling of utter conviction; nor are we asking whether a judgment made at a given moment can be withdrawn at that same moment. We are talking of knowledge without possibility of error—or, in practice, of judgment immune to subsequent withdrawal for cause. I cannot be said to be certain about what occurs at a given moment, even at that moment, if I may justifiably change my mind about it at a later moment.

The advocate of empirical certainty, however, is not put off by a failure to find instances or by the problems encountered in arriving at an unexceptionable statement of his thesis. The difficulty of formulating the given must not, Mr. Lewis[1] warns, lead us to suppose that there is no given; for if there were no given there would be no experience as we know it at all. No argument can erase the fact that experience and knowledge are not purely arbitrary, willful inventions. The sheer stubbornness of experience recognized by even

---

[1] [This article was printed as one of a series of three articles on the topic of certainty. The other two are by C. I. Lewis and Hans Reichenbach.—Editor]

the most thoroughgoing idealists is proof enough that there is *something there* in experience, some element not manufactured but given. This cannot be denied whatever may be the difficulties of articulating it.

But this all seems to me to point to, or at least to be compatible with, the conclusion that while something is given, nothing given is true; that while some things may be indubitable, nothing is certain. What we have been urged to grant amounts at most to this: materials for our particles of experience are given, sensory qualities or events or other elements are not created at will but presented, experience has some content even though our description of it may be artificial or wrong and even though the precise differentiation between what is given and what is not given may be virtually impossible. But to such content or materials or particles or elements, the terms "true," "false," and "certain" are quite inapplicable. These elements are simply there or not there. To grant that some are there is not to grant that anything is certain. Such elements may be indubitable in the vacuous sense that doubt is irrelevant to them, as it is to a desk; but they, like the desk, are equally devoid of certainty. They may be before us, but they are neither true nor false. For truth and falsity and certainty pertain to statements or judgments and not to mere particles or materials or elements. Thus, to deny that there are empirical certainties does not imply that experience is a pure fiction, that it is without content, or even that there is no given element.

Some of Mr. Lewis' arguments, however, are aimed directly at showing that there must be some indubitable judgments or statements, not merely that there is something presented. Unless some statements are certain, he argues, none is even probable. Mr. Reichenbach has disputed this argument on mathematical grounds, but perhaps Mr. Lewis intends only to make a somewhat less technical point. It plainly does us no good to know that a statement is probable with respect to certain premises unless we have some confidence in these premises. And we cannot just say that the premises themselves need merely be probable; for this means only that they in turn are probable with respect to other premises, and so on without end. Probability will be genuinely useful in judging the truth of sentences—the argument runs—only if the chain of probability relationships is somewhere moored to certainty. This is closely akin to the argument against a pure coherence theory of truth. Internal coherence is obviously a necessary but not a sufficient condition for the truth of a system; for we need also some means of choosing between equally tight systems that are incompatible with each other. There must be a tie to fact through, it is contended, some immediately certain statements. Otherwise compatibility with a system is not even a probable indication of the truth of any statement.

Now clearly we cannot suppose that statements derive their credibility from other statements without ever bringing this string of statements to earth. Credibility may be transmitted from one statement to another through deductive or probability connections; but credibility does not spring from these connections by spontaneous generation. Somewhere along the line some statements, whether atomic sense reports or the entire system or something in between, must have initial credibility. So far the argument is sound. To use the term "probability" for this initial credibility is to risk misunderstanding since probability, strictly speaking, is not initial at all but always relative to specified premises. Yet all that is indicated is credibility to some degree, not certainty. To say that some statements must be initially credible if any statement is ever to be credible at all is not to say that any statement is immune to withdrawal. For indeed, as remarked earlier, no matter how strong its initial claim to preservation may be, a statement will be dropped if its retention —along with consequent adjustments in the interest of coherence— results in a system that does not satisfy as well as possible the totality of claims presented by all relevant statements. In the "search for truth" we deal with the clamoring demands of conflicting statements by trying, so to speak, to realize the greatest happiness of the greatest number of them. These demands constitute a different factor from coherence, the wanted means of choosing between different systems, the missing link with fact; yet none is so strong that it may not be denied. That we have probable knowledge, then, implies no certainty but only initial credibility.

Still, I am not satisfied that we have as yet gone to the heart of the matter. Just why is it so important to decide whether or not there is some empirical certainty? Mr. Reichenbach says that Mr. Lewis' view is a vestige of rationalism; but unlike the rationalists, Mr. Lewis obviously is not seeking certainties in order to use them as axioms for a philosophical system. If he could once prove that there are some empirical certainties, I doubt if he would be much disposed to go catch one. Rather he is convinced that such certainties are somehow essential to knowledge as we possess it. And I suspect that both his specific arguments and my counterarguments may leave him, as they leave me, with a feeling that the real issue has not yet been brought into relief. The underlying motivation for Mr. Lewis's whole argument is to be found, I think, in the problem of relating language to what it describes.

Consider the familiar problem faced by a common version of pragmatism. The meaning and truth of a statement are said to lie in its predictive consequences. These consequences are themselves statements; for from statements we can deduce, or even infer with probability, nothing but other statements. But, if the truth of these predictions depends in turn upon the truth of others derived from them, we are lost in an endless regress. The theory rests upon our being able, when a particular moment arrives, to decide with some degree of confidence whether a prediction made concerning that moment is or is not fulfilled. Accordingly, statements describing immediate experience are specifically exempted from the predictive criterion. But what, then, is to be said concerning them? What sort of relationship to experience makes such a statement true or credible? The connection between a statement and the very dissimilar experience it describes is not easy to grasp. Testimony to the rather mysterious character of the relation is found in the oblique way it is referred to in the literature. Mr. Quine wrote recently that a system of statements "impinges at its edges" upon experience; and he has been twitted for waxing so metaphorical. I suspect that the metaphorical term was chosen purposely to intimate that we have here an inadequately understood relationship. Again, Mr. Lewis, choosing simile rather than metaphor, merely likens the relationship to that between an outcry and the fearful apparition that evokes it.

What I am suggesting is that Mr. Lewis is actually more vitally concerned with the directness and immediacy and irreducibility of this relation between sensory experience and sentences describing it than with the certainty of these sentences. For, if this crucial relation seems inexplicable, perhaps—the thought runs—that is just because it is so fundamental and simple as to require no explanation. Learning a language may involve becoming acquainted with this elementary and irreducible relation, of which subsequent cases are instantly recognized. The claim that statements describing bare sense experience are certain then becomes an accidental by-product of the view that their truth is immediately and directly apprehended. And the real challenge that emerges is not to muster arguments showing that there are no empirical certainties, but to point a way of explaining the root relation between language and the nonlinguistic experience it describes.

Plainly we cannot look to resemblance for any help. The English statement "There is a blue patch" and its Chinese equivalent are very unlike, and both are even more unlike the blue patch itself. In no literal sense does language mirror experience. Yet this false start has something in its favor. The explanation in terms of resemblance is very good except for being so wrong. By that I mean that to explain the relation in question is to subsume it under or analyze it into more general relations. Such terms as "describes," "is true," "denotes," and "designates," require explanation because they are idiosyncratic to cases where the first element in question is linguistic. Only words and strings of words denote or are true. Our problem is to reduce these purely semantic predicates to predicates that have familiar instances in nonlinguistic experience.[2]

A clue to a better starting point than resemblance lies in the fact that a toot may warn of an oncoming train or that a ray of dawn foretells the approach of daylight. Here are nonverbal events standing as *signals* for others. In like fashion two sensory experiences or phenomena are often such that the earlier is a promise or warning or signal of the later. A feeling of warmth may signal the imminent appearance of a fiery red patch in the visual field; an evenly shaded patch may signal a certain tactual experience to come. Of course, the situation is seldom quite so simple. More often, an isolated presentation signals another only conditionally upon certain behavior; that is, the tactual experience ensues only if I reach out my hand in a certain way. But this can be accommodated without difficulty merely by recognizing that a presentation is itself usually a partial, incomplete signal that combines with other presentations (such as those of bodily movements) to constitute a signal for a subsequent experience. In other words, a signal is often comprised of more than

---

[2] Thus our problem differs from that considered by Tarski in *Der Wahrheitsbegriff in den formalisierten Sprachen,* in which he defines truth in terms of the purely semantic notion of *satisfaction*.

one presentation; but this does not affect the important point that some nonlinguistic experiences function as signals.

If asked for a psychological account of signaling, we might say that the earlier experience arouses an expectation that is fulfilled, or a tension that is released, by the later one. But this and the various questions it inspires are not quite apposite to the present task. Our primary objective is not to explain this relation but to explain certain semantic predicates in terms of it. So long as we are satisfied that the relation clearly obtains in nonlinguistic experience, we can postpone consideration of its anatomy and genealogy.

If experiences comprised of such presentations as shaded patches can signal, there is no mystery about how an irregular black patch or a brief stretch of sound may function in the same way. And a statement-event,[3] or other string of word-events, is simply some such patch or stretch. Just as a blue patch and some kinaesthetic presentations may signal the coming appearance of a red patch, so also does a statement-event—let us name it *"F"*—saying in advance that there will be a red patch in the visual field at the time in question, *t*. Statements are merely more complicated, and hence often more specific, than some other signals. It is clear enough how a signaling system can be elaborated and refined, once even a few signaling relationships are available. Under some circumstances or other, almost anything can be made to serve as a signal for almost any subsequent experience. Differentiation between conditioned and unconditioned signaling is irrelevant to our present purpose.

It may be contended that statements signal by virtue of their meaning, and that their signaling is thus essentially different from that of nonlinguistic elements. On the contrary, I should say rather that statements mean by virtue of their signaling; for "means," like "denotes," is one of the puzzling semantic predicates that constitute our problem. Yet this is not to say that a statement either means or denotes what it signals; the explanation of meaning or denoting in terms of signaling would have to be much more complex than that.

So far, however, only statements like *F* that are in the future tense have been provided for. What are we to do about statements in the present tense? Suppose the statement *P* "There is now a red patch in the visual field" occurs at the time *t* above in question. *P* does not

---

[3] I use the term "statement-event" at times to emphasize that I think of a statement as an actual uterance or inscription-at-a-moment.

signal the simultaneous occurrence of the red patch; for signaling is always forecasting. Nevertheless, we know that P is true if and only if F is true. Hence P is true just in case F is a genuine signal. Although P does not itself signal the occurrence of the red patch, the truth of P is explained in terms of the truth of the earlier statement F, which does signal this occurrence. Statements in the past tense can be handled in the same way as those in the present tense; and tenseless statements, depending on whether they occur before, during, or after the time they pertain to, in the same way as statements in, respectively, the future, present, and past tense. A key point of the present proposal lies in its radical departure from the usual attack, which rests the truth of all statements upon that of statements in the present tense and leaves us at a loss to deal with these. After all, a thoroughly predictive theory can be carried through only by basing all truth upon the truth of statement-events concerning later events.

What I have been saying is meant to apply just to rather simple statements, like those illustrated, about phenomena. The relation of other statements to these is not part of my present problem. But even with respect to the simple statements in question, a number of problems must be left untouched. For example, I cannot here discuss the means available for dealing with a statement, in the present tense, such that no correlative statement in the future tense ever happened to occur.

I expect to be told that what I offer is a fragment of a time-worn theory in a somewhat topsy-turvy version. But I make no claim to a complete or unprecedented or pretty theory. Nor am I at all complacent about pragmatic-predictive epistemology in general. What I have tried to do here is to suggest how, in terms of a pragmatism not entirely alien to Mr. Lewis' point of view, the connection between language and what it describes may be given a reasonable explanation. In that case, this relation need no longer be regarded as immediate, mystic, and inexplicable. And this, if I am correct, will remove the last and deepest motivation for the defense of empirical certainty.

Bibliographical Essay

This bibliography is a selective guide for further explorations into the problems discussed in this volume. There are established classics in the history of philosophy. In ancient philosophy, Plato's dialogue *Theaetetus* should be consulted for the problem of providing a definition of knowledge; it is translated with a running commentary by F. M. CORNFORD in his *Plato's Theory of Knowledge* (London: Routledge & Kegan Paul Ltd. 1935), which also includes a translation of and commentary on Plato's *Sophist*. Among Aristotle's writings the most directly relevant is his *Posterior Analytics* which is included in a handy volume of his works, *The Basic Works of Aristotle*, edited by RICHARD MCKEON (New York: Random House, Inc. 1941).

In modern philosophy, the most important work in the rationalist tradition is Descartes' *Meditations on First Philosophy*; a standard translation is in HALDANE and ROSS, *The Philosophical Works of Descartes* (Cambridge University Press, 1931), which also includes in the second volume the "Objections Urged against the *Meditations*" and DESCARTES's "Replies." The British empiricist tradition can best be approached through JOHN LOCKE's *An Essay Concerning Human Understanding*; there is a well annotated edition by ALEXANDER CAMPBELL FRASER (New York: Dover Publications, Inc., 1959) and a useful abridged edition by A. S. PRINGLE-PATTISON (Oxford University Press, 1924). Berkeley's version of empiricism is contained in three important words—*An Essay towards a New Theory of Vision, A Treatise concerning the Principles of Human Knowledge,* and *Three Dialogues between Hylas and Philonous*—all of which are contained in M. W. CALKINS, editor, *Berkeley: Selections* (New York: Charles Scribner's Sons, 1929). DAVID HUME's version of empiricism is contained in his *A Treatise of Human Nature, Book I* and his *An Enquiry concerning Human Understanding.* In his *New Essays concerning Human Understanding*, translated by A. G. LANGLEY (La Salle, Illinois: Open Court Publishing Co., 1949), G. W. LEIBNIZ provides a running commentary and critique of Locke's *Essay.* Thomas Reid's *Essays on the Intellectual Powers of Man* is contained in the first volume of Reid's *Philosophical Works* edited by SIR WILLIAM HAMILTON (1846); an abridged edition was prepared by A. D. WOOZLEY (London: Macmillan & Co. Ltd., 1941). Finally, for Immanuel Kant's *Critique of Pure Reason* the recommended translation is that of NORMAN KEMP SMITH (New York: St. Martin's Press, Inc., 1965); the *Critique,* which is an especially difficult work, may be approached through Kant's own brief statement of its leading ideas in his *Prolegomena to any Future Metaphysics.*

The list of contemporary writings shall be restricted to major books. Three of A. J. Ayer's books are worthy of mention. His *Language, Truth and Logic* (London: Victor Gollancz Ltd., 1936) is a classic defense of logical positivism; his *Foundations of Empirical Knowledge* (London: Macmillan & Co. Ltd., 1940) is a major presentation of phenomenalism; and his *The Problem of Knowledge* (London: Macmillan and Penguin Books, 1956) is an excellent survey of some major problems of epistemology. Ayer's *Foundations* is the subject of a penetrating criticism by J. L. AUSTIN in his *Sense and Sensibilia* (Oxford University Press, 1962).

In the tradition of analytic philosophy the writings of G. E. MOORE and BERTRAND RUSSELL are indispensable. In MOORE's *Philosophical Papers* (London: George Allen and Unwin Ltd., 1959) his influential common sense approach is stated in the essays "A Defense of Common Sense," "Proof of an External World," "Four Forms of Scepticism," and "Certainty." MOORE's *Philosophical Studies* (London: Routledge and Kegan Paul, 1922) contains his early essays on perception, including his famous criticism of Berkeley "The Refutation of Idealism." Among RUSSELL's many books those especially worthy of mention are *The Problems of Philosophy* (Oxford University Press, 1912), *Our Knowledge of the External World* (2nd ed.), (New York: W. W. Norton & Co., Inc., 1929), *An*

Inquiry into Meaning and Truth (New York: W. W. Norton & Co., Inc., 1940), and *Human Knowledge: Its Scope and Limits* (New York: Simon and Schuster, Inc., 1948). In the tradition of ordinary language analysis, GILBERT RYLE's *The Concept of Mind* (London: Hutchinson's University Library, 1949) contains important discussions of knowledge and perception. LUDWIG WITTGENSTEIN's *Philosophical Investigations* (Oxford: Basil Blackwell, 1953) provides criticisms of traditional approaches in epistemology based on a new theory of language. NORMAN MALCOLM's collection of essays on such topics as knowledge, verification, perception, and memory, *Knowledge and Certainty* (Englewood Cliffs, N.J.: Prentice-Hall, Inc., 1965) is written under the influence of Wittgenstein.

In the tradition of American pragmatism, a useful collection containing the major essays of Charles S. Peirce is *Values in a Universe of Chance* edited by PHILIP WIENER (New York: Doubleday, 1958). *The Writings of William James* edited by JOHN J. McDERMOTT includes James's important writings in epistemology *Pragmatism* and *Essays in Radical Empiricism*. John Dewey's epistemology is most thoroughly developed in his *Logic, the Theory of Inquiry* (New York: Henry Holt, 1938).

The basic source of contemporary phenomenology is EDMUND HUSSERL's *Ideas, General Introduction to Pure Phenomenology* translated by W. R. Boyce Gibson (New York: The Macmillan Co., 1931). MERLEAU-PONTY's *Phenomenology of Perception* translated by Colin Smith (London: Routledge and Kegan Paul, 1962) is another major contribution to this movement.

A number of other books and authors should be mentioned. BRAND BLANSHARD's *The Nature of Thought* (London: George Allen and Unwin Ltd., 1939) is an unusually clear and well-argued presentation of a point of view in the tradition of British Idealism; it contains a critical survey of many important twentieth-century theories of knowledge. Blanshard has brought his criticism of analytic philosophy up to date in his *Reason and Analysis* (La Salle, Illinois: Open Court Publishing Co., 1962). C. D. BROAD's *The Mind and its Place in Nature* (London: Routledge & Kegan Paul Ltd., 1925) contains suggestive and incisive discussions of perception, memory, introspection, and knowledge of other minds. ERNST CASSIRER's *The Philosophy of Symbolic Forms* (New Haven: Yale University Press, 1957) is an attempt to apply the insights of Kant's epistemology to the topics of language, myth, and knowledge. RODERICK M. CHISHOLM's *Perceiving: a Philosophical Study* (Ithaca: Cornell University Press, 1957) has occasioned a great deal of comment and discussion; his survey of epistemology *The Theory of Knowledge* (Englewood Cliffs, N.J.: Prentice-Hall, Inc., 1966) is both penetrating and original. Two books by C. I. LEWIS are worthy of note; in his *Mind and the World Order* (New York: Charles Scribner's Sons, 1929) he attempts to reconcile pragmatism and Kant; in his *An Analysis of Knowledge and Valuation* his theories of a priori and empirical knowledge are developed at greater length. ARTHUR LOVEJOY's *The Revolt Against Dualism* (La Salle, Illinois: Open Court Publishing Co., 1929) is a vigorous defense of the representative theory of perception against its modern critics.

Several collections of articles and excerpts are useful for the bibliographies they contain. For a bibliography on logical positivism see *Logical Positivism,* edited by A. J. AYER (Glencoe, Illinois: The Free Press, 1959). For one on pragmatism see *Pragmatic Philosophy,* edited by AMELIE RORTY (Garden City, N.Y.: Doubleday & Company, Inc., 1966). Bibliographical references on phenomenology and on the American and British realist movement are given in *Realism and the Background of Phenomenology* edited by RODERICK M. CHISHOLM (Glencoe, Illinois: The Free Press, 1960). References on the problem of defining knowledge are contained in *Knowledge and Belief,* edited by A. PHILLIPS GRIFFITHS (Oxford University Press, 1967).